Arab Development Funds in the Middle East

(PPS-19)

Pergamon Titles of Related Interest

Amos   Arab-Israeli Military/Political Relations: Arab
Perceptions and the Politics of Escalation

Feld/Boyd   Comparative Regional Systems: West and East
Europe, North America, The Middle East and Developing
Countries

Francisco/Laird/Laird   The Political Economy of Collectivized
Agriculture: A Comparative Study of Communist and Non-
Communist Systems

Franko/Seiber   Developing Country Debt

Freedman   World Politics and the Arab-Israeli Conflict

Golany   Arid Zone Settlement Planning: The Israeli Experience

Grieves   Transnationalism in World Politics and Business

Leitenberg/Sheffer   Great Power Intervention in the Middle East

PERGAMON
POLICY
STUDIES

Arab Development Funds in the Middle East

Soliman Demir

Published for UNITAR

Pergamon Press

NEW YORK • OXFORD • TORONTO • SYDNEY • FRANKFURT • PARIS

Pergamon Press Offices:

U.S.A.   Pergamon Press Inc., Maxwell House, Fairview Park,
                     Elmsford, New York 10523, U.S.A.

U.K.   Pergamon Press Ltd., Headington Hill Hall,
                     Oxford OX3 0BW, England

CANADA   Pergamon of Canada Ltd., 150 Consumers Road,
                     Willowdale, Ontario M2J 1P9, Canada

AUSTRALIA   Pergamon Press (Aust) Pty. Ltd., P O Box 544,
                     Potts Point, NSW 2011, Australia

FRANCE   Pergamon Press SARL, 24 rue des Ecoles,
                     75240 Paris, Cedex 05, France

FEDERAL REPUBLIC Pergamon Press GmbH, 6242 Kronberg/Taunus,
OF GERMANY   Pferdstrasse 1, Federal Republic of Germany

Contents

List of Figures and Tables

Members of Review Panel

H.E. Dr. Ahmed Esmat Abdel-Meguid	Permanent Representative of Egypt to the United Nations
Mr. Abdullah Abdullarham	Permanent Mission of the United Arab Emirates to the United Nations
Mr. Basil Al-Bustany	Adviser to Executive Director, the World Bank
Mr. Taher Al-Hussamy	Permanent Mission of Syrian Arab Republic to the United Nations
Mr. Sharaf Al-Saidi	Permanent Mission of the Yemen Arab Republic to the United Nations
Mr. Mickhail S. Amirdzhanov	Permanent Mission of the USSR to the United Nations
Mr. Hatem Bergaoui	Permanent Mission of Tunisia to the United Nations
Mr. Frank Brecher	Permanent Mission of the United States of America to the United Nations
Mr. Andrew Cordery	Permanent Mission of the United Kingdom to the United Nations
H.E. Mr. Abdulmohsen H. El-Jeaan	Deputy Permanent Representative of Kuwait to the United Nations
H.E. Dr. Ali Humaidan	Permanent Representative of the United Arab Emirates to the United Nations
Mr. James T. Ivy	The Ford Foundation
Mr. Elmore Jackson	The Aspen Institute
Mr. Souheil Khauly	Permanent Mission of Qatar to the United Nations
Ms. Bernadette Lefort	Permanent Mission of France to the United Nations
H.E. Dr. Hazem Nuseibeh	Permanent Representative of Jordan to the United Nations
Mr. Mubarak H. Rahamtalla	Acting Consul General, the Sudanese Consulate General in New York

ix

Mr. Mohammed Taher Edeed

Permanent Mission of Oman to the
United Nations

UNITAR

Dr. Davidson Nicol   Executive Director
Mr. Robert Jordan   Director of Research
Mr. Abdul-Ghani Al-Rafei   Director of Training
Mr. Soliman Demir   Research Associate

Preface

In the light of various General Assembly resolutions of the sixth and seventh special sessions, the wishes of the UNITAR Board of Trustees, and a major United Nations concern with issues related to a new international economic order, the UNITAR research program increasingly emphasizes studies on economic and technical cooperation among developing countries and the relations between the developed North and the developing South.

This volume deals with the efforts of three Arab development funds in promoting economic cooperation and development within the Arab region. Similar UNITAR studies of other developing regions in Africa and Latin America are being undertaken.

In this study, Dr. Soliman Demir, the author, analyzes the organizational setup and development policies of three major Arab development organizations: the Kuwait Fund for Arab Economic Development (established in 1961), the Abu Dhabi Fund for Arab Economic Development (1971), and the Arab Fund for Economic and Social Development (1972). After identifying the characteristics of each fund in dealing with its designated tasks, the author discusses how the three funds cooperate and the potential for increased cooperation in the future. Cooperation between the funds as a group and the various United Nations organizations both within and outside the Arab region is reported in the final part of the study. The discussion stresses the role that the funds and the United Nations organizations could play in promoting a coordinated regional strategy for Arab economic and social development.

In accordance with UNITAR practice, an earlier draft of this study was reviewed by the diplomats, international officials, and scholars whose names are listed on page ix. This final version has benefited from their observations and suggestions, as well as from comments received from the three Arab funds.

Dr. Demir is a member of the Research Department of UNITAR. His area of specialization is the political economy of development, with particular emphasis on the Arab region.

The views and conclusions in this study are the responsibility of the author and do not necessarily reflect the opinions of the Board of Trustees or officials of UNITAR. Although UNITAR takes no position on the views and conclusions expressed by the authors of its studies, it does assume responsibility for determining whether a study merits publication and dissemination.

We are pleased to publish this study by Dr. Demir.

Davidson Nicol
Executive Director

Acknowledgments

I am grateful to the Abu Dhabi, Arab, and Kuwait funds for providing detailed comments on an earlier draft of this study. Many other experts have generously extended comments and suggestions that were invaluable to me in preparing the final version of the study. In particular, I would like to thank Dr. Ibrahim Shihata, director general of OPEC Special Fund, Dr. Joseph Grunwald of the Brookings Institution, and Professor Georges Abi-Saab, of the Graduate Institute of International Studies in Geneva; their comments and suggestions have greatly improved this work. The responsibility for all errors in fact or judgment is, of course, mine.

Introduction

This report covers three Arab development funds in the Middle East: the Kuwait Fund for Arab Economic Development (1961), the Abu Dhabi Fund for Arab Economic Development (established in 1971), and the Arab Fund for Economic and Social Development (established by an international agreement in 1968 that came into effect in 1972). These three development funds endeavor to promote regional development in the Arab world. The first two were established by their respective governments to administer economic aid to other Arab governments. Their initial mandates covered only the Arab region. In 1974, the Kuwait government and then the Government of the United Arab Emirates (Abu Dhabi) modified the laws governing the activities of the two funds to permit the two financial institutions to expand their lending operations to all developing countries in Africa, Asia, and Latin America. The Arab Fund continued to maintain its regional nature as a multilateral financial institution geared to the service of its member states. In this way the Arab Fund is similar to the Asian, African, or Inter-American Development Banks.

The purpose of this research is to study the efforts the three Arab funds have made to promote development in their region. Special emphasis is given to the interaction among the three financial institutions in their endeavors to promote regional development. We are also concerned with means to promote cooperative relationships among the funds and other international organizations within the United Nations system.(1)

Although government decisions in both Abu Dhabi and Kuwait have expanded the funds' sphere of operations, all the loans and technical assistance of the Abu Dhabi Fund until the end of 1975 went to Arab countries. The Kuwait Fund is expected to continue to devote a substantial part of its resources to the Arab region.(2) The Arab Fund concentrates exclusively, by its mandate, on the Arab region. Indeed, the surge in the financial reserves of some Arab countries (especially Saudi Arabia, Kuwait, and Abu Dhabi) raises hopes for a more concentrated and integrated effort to develop the Arab region.(3)

xv

Hopes for a more effective regional development in the Middle East coincide with a more generic process to establish a "new international economic order," which has been taking place on the international level under United Nations auspices. Upon the initiative of the late President Boumedienne of Algeria, the United Nations General Assembly met in its sixth special session in May 1974 to discuss efforts to establish a more equitable economic relationship between the industrialized developed countries and the developing countries. These efforts continued later in September 1975 when the seventh special session of the General Assembly met to discuss the "Establishment of a New International Economic Order."(4)

The process of negotiating NIEO takes place in a variety of United Nations forums. The calls for the establishment of NIEO and the subsequent efforts by the international community to accommodate the desires and demands of the developing countries were brought about by a sudden improvement in the negotiating capabilities of the developing countries. This improvement was made possible through the actions of the Organization of Petroleum Exporting Countries (OPEC) in 1973 and 1974. The drastic increases in oil prices during 1973-74, what some call the OPEC revolution,(5) have demonstrated that a group of developing countries is capable of effecting significant changes in international economic relationships. The actions of OPEC imparted a new strength to the negotiating positions of the developing countries. These actions also resulted in the emergence of some oil-rich developing countries as aid-donors on a scale unknown before.(6)

This report is a study of the institutional arrangements through which some developing countries perform the role of aid donors. It deals with the efforts of two such countries   (Kuwait and Abu Dhabi)   to administer their aid to the Arab region through national institutions. It also deals with the efforts of both capital-surplus and capital-deficit Arab countries when they combine their resources in an institutional form (the Arab Fund) to promote the development of their region. As indicated earlier, these efforts in regional development occur in the context of a larger global process that aims at the creation of a new international economic order. A successful model for regional cooperation can enhance our knowledge of the conditions under which fruitful cooperation on the international level could be achieved. This is especially true because development on the regional level would have to face and solve problems that lie at the heart of global cooperation: i.e., transfer of resources, the development of appropriate technology, and the use of financial resources to improve the productive capabilities of the countries in the region.

In the field of development, there is always a need to try new initiatives, "as one after another of the 'keys' to development fails to open the door."(7) In this study we shall try to delineate the elements of a regional strategy in which the Arab funds under study could play an important role. The strategy is guided by the results of past experiences in the Arab region and is inspired by the major concerns of the developing countries as expressed in various international forums.(8)

A note on the data presented in this study is in order. The reader will notice that the availability of data (as expressed in the various tables and charts) is not the same for each. Data shown in the various tables are not strictly comparable for the three funds for two reasons. As the lifespans of the three funds differ, the amounts of historical data on the funds differs. Two of the funds (Abu Dhabi and Kuwait) are national aid agencies, while the Arab Fund is a multilateral aid agency. This fact reflects on how each fund represents its data and also on the range of activities each fund undertakes, as we describe in this study.

METHODOLOGY

The research for this study was conducted in Kuwait and Abu Dhabi in early 1976. Information is based on official documents of the development funds, policy statements and papers, both published and unpublished, internal memorandums made available to us, and interviews with a representative sample of both management and technical staff of the funds under study. A total of sixteen interviews was conducted: five in Abu Dhabi, five at the Kuwait Fund, and six at the Arab Fund.(9) An effort was made to insure that the interviews cover the different organizational departments of the funds and the various technical expertise represented in their professional staffs.

In the next three chapters we deal with the Kuwait Fund, the Abu Dhabi Fund, and the Arab Fund, in that order. In the fourth chapter we deal with the interrelationships among the three funds, their cooperation with international organizations working in the field of development, and particularly, their role as a component of regional development strategy.

1 Kuwait Fund For Arab Economic Development

The Kuwait Fund was established in 1961 (Law No. 35), the same year that Kuwait gained independence and full sovereignty. The oldest national development aid agency in the Arab world, the fund was emulated later by Abu Dhabi, Iraq, and Saudi Arabia. The circumstances in which the Fund was established indicate that the policy makers in the newly independent state wished to present to the world in general and to the Arab countries in particular an image of Kuwait as a responsible member in the international community, one ready to use its wealth to help others.(1)

Since the Fund began operations and until 1974, it concentrated its aid activities exclusively on Arab countries. This led some to view the process of creating the fund as political, and its role in transferring economic benefits to other Arab countries as necessary to preserve Kuwait's independence and autonomy in the Arab region.(2) The Kuwait Fund, indeed, represented an organizational innovation as a national economic aid agency. It was established as a public corporation with autonomous legal status to ensure smoothness of operations and continuity in policies, not possible under different organizational structures.

Compared with national aid agencies in other donor countries, such as the United States, France, Britain, and Sweden, the Kuwait Fund has the advantage of continuity in its policies and the fairly certain flow of funds through capitalization. Annual budgetary debates on foreign policy and other political considerations play a less important role in an organizational structure such as the Kuwait Fund than they do in the aid agencies of the United States, Canada, France, or Britain. The reason is the relatively autonomous position of the fund among governmental institutions in Kuwait, and the availability of resources that the Fund's capital guarantees.

In the following two sections, we describe the management of the Kuwait Fund and its policies and operations.

THE MANAGEMENT OF THE KUWAIT FUND

The Kuwait Fund is administered by a board of directors and a director general. The board of directors is "the highest authority"(3) of the fund in terms of policy guidance; it is the ultimate overseer of the fund's operations. The director general is the administrative head of the fund who is responsible for its day-to-day management.(4)

The Board of Directors

The board of directors consists of eight Kuwaiti nationals of "recognized competence." It is chaired by the prime minister, who appoints members of the board for a term of two years, subject to renewal.

According to the fund's charters, the board of directors is entrusted with the following functions:

1. Consider and decide, upon the recommendation of the director general, on proposed loans and other forms of assistance to Arab and other developing states.

2. Determine the form and terms for the participation of the fund in the development projects and programs of Arab and other developing states.

3. Approve the amount of loans and other kinds of assistance.

4. Determine the general policy of investments by the fund and the forms of such investments.

5. Authorize the borrowings of the fund and determine the amounts and terms of such borrowings.

6. Lay down the staff regulations and supervise the application of such regulations.

7. Approve the administrative budget and the closing accounts of the fund.

8. Appoint the fund's auditors and determine their remuneration.

From the fund's beginning in 1962 and until 1974, the chairman of the board of directors was the minister of oil and finance ex officio. Although Law 25 (1974) stipulates that the prime minister is to become the chairman of the board, Article 29 of the fund's charter states that the prime minister may delegate all or part of his powers to the minister of finance and oil. Indeed, this has been the practice, and the minister of finance continues to assume the same functions in regard to the fund as before the enactment of Law 25 (1974).

Most members of the board of directors are Kuwaiti businessmen, unlike the Abu Dhabi Fund, whose board of directors is dominated by cabinet members.   This difference signifies the special characteristics of Kuwait among the Arab Gulf states. Earlier than other Gulf Emirates, Kuwait has developed a strong and articulate business community based on trade with neighboring countries and with such distant countries as India and Pakistan. The interests of the business community are aptly represented in the fund board of directors. The role and, consequently, the influence of the business community is expeced to increase in the coming years when the interests of the business community become more articulated with the development of the banking system and the financial markets in Kuwait.

Political considerations signify another element in the composition of the board of directors. The chairman, whether it be the minister of finance or the prime minister, ensures that the political interests of the state are considered in the fund's policies and operations. The present composition of the board ensures that the policies and operations of the fund have the backing of the business groups in Kuwait in addition to the government's approval.

As in most similar organizations, the role of the board in policy initiation and development is not tremendous. Instead the prominent role of the board is in policy legitimization, which is necessary for the effective performance of the fund.

The board meets four times a year and makes decisions by a majority vote, except in special cases. For example, a two-thirds majority is needed to approve a project loan that is more than 50% of the total cost of such a project.

The director general attends board meetings and participates in the deliberations, but does not have the right to vote.

The Director General

The charter of the Kuwait Fund states that the director general has the direct responsibility for all administrative, financial, and technical matters in the fund. He also represents the fund in official dealings with other institutions and courts of law.

The director general is specifically entrusted with the following functions:

1. Implement the resolutions of the board of directors.

2. Prepare and submit to the board of directors the proposed administrative budget and the closing account.

3. Authorize expenditures within the limits of the administrative budget.

4. Submit an annual report to the board of directors on the progress of work in the fund, including financial statements certified by auditors and a detailed account of the activities of the fund during the preceding financial year.

5. Receive and appraise applications for loans and financial and technical assistance, and submit appropriate recommendations to the board of directors.

6. Implement loan and other agreements to provide assistance from the fund to its clients.

Abdlatif Al-Hamad has been the director general of the Kuwait Fund since 1963. No doubt the fund's development through the years has been very much influenced by his personality and ideas. It is also true that the leadership role played by the director general has enabled the Kuwait Fund to maintain high professional standards in its work through the recruitment of highly qualified professionals from the various Arab countries.

As head of the fund's management, the director general plays an important role in policy development for the fund; a review of major policy and task decisions indicates that fund management played the leading role in initiating policy.(5)

Besides managing Kuwait's agency for foreign aid, the director general engages in other activities that reflect favorably on the Kuwait Fund as a prominent Arab development institution (e.g., being a member of the board of trustees of the Institute of Palestinian Studies, and one of the constituent members of the Center for Arab Studies, an institute dedicated to policy research in cultural, social, economic, and political fields to promote Arab integration).

In describing the role of the Kuwait Fund in the context of Kuwait policies toward the Arab region, Al-Hamad indicated that "we believe that the socio-economic underdevelopment in the Arab world cannot be conquered without the collaborated efforts of the Arab nation . . . the Kuwait Fund is in fact part of these efforts. Arab monies and efforts in the service of a better future for the Arab individual."(6)

Internal Organization

According to one account, a total of three employees, including the director general, ran the Kuwait Fund in its early years.(7) The Kuwait Fund has been known, since its inception, to avoid inflated administrative edifices and to pursue cautious personnel policies. It has tried to avoid such practices as overstaffing and fondness for elaborate procedural and administrative routines, which are common to all bureaucracies, especially those in developing countries. Al-Hamad wrote in 1971, "We are very careful not to slip into bureaucratization . . . this (mistake) is easy to commit because we are an agency that offers services to an extended geographical area, the Arab region, that consists of independent entities . . . we are careful to build an organization of a limited size that consists of a few selected Arab citizens . . . in our work quality always supersedes quantity."(8)

Such a statement reveals an organizational approach that influences the fund's recruitment and personnel policies, internal organization, and task-fulfillment practices.

The recruitment policy of the fund is based on selecting only highly qualified senior professionals in fields relevant to the fund's work. Such senior professionals are usually non-Kuwaiti Arabs. The fund recruits young Kuwaiti nationals who are expected to develop career objectives and to assume more managerial responsibilities. There are 17 Kuwaiti professional staff members in the fund (excluding the director general and his deputy), with specializations in economics, law, and financial analysis. There are also 19 non-Kuwaiti professional staff members, of whom 12 hold doctorates in such fields as economics, law, finance, and engineering.(9)

The internal organization of the fund is not based on clear-cut criteria such as functional or geographical lines. For the first twelve years of the fund's operations there were no department heads. The work was conducted on a task-oriented basis. Decisions on forming loan appraisal teams or missions to borrowing countries were all made by the director general. The professional staff, especially the senior members, formed a pool of expertise from which to draw those best qualified for the task at hand. Decisions on who should attend meetings, represent the fund at international gatherings, and negotiate with other lending institutions were based on who was available at the time. When the fund was young, and small in terms of staff members and tasks to be handled, this mode of operations offered flexibility and enabled the fund to respond on short notice to the demands of the work. It also enabled the fund to keep its administrative expenses to a minimum.

In 1974, when the Kuwait government decided to increase the capital of the fund to one billion Kuwaiti dinar (KD=$3.55) and to broaden the geographical scope of its operations to cover developing countries in Asia, Africa, and Latin America, it became obvious that the fund would have to change its pattern of organization to cope with the enlarged demands. Expansion meant changing to a larger organization. For the fund, this entailed changing from a flexible family-type structure, where interpersonal relations play a significant role, to a bureaucratic structure,(10) where rules and regulations are more significant in determining organizational behavior and task assignment.

The present organization of the fund may be viewed as a transition stage. The older pattern of a flexible, almost rules-free organizational structure would probably be transformed into one elaborate enough to accommodate a volume of operations commensurate with $3.55 billion in capital, and a geographical coverage of Asia, Africa and Latin America. The expanded organizational structure would have to meet such requirements as 1) a well-designed recuitment policy to cope with diversification of staff in specializations and skills as needed for enlarged operations; 2) selection of certain criteria for internal organization on functional lines or geographical lines, or a balanced combination of both; 3) an elaborate decision structure to resolve policy debates, which would be inevitable in such a large organization. The expansion of operations would require a wide spectrum of professional inputs in order to settle policy questions. In a large professional organization, which the fund is bound to be, informed policy decisions would be difficult to reach in a structure where top management relies on limited sources for arriving at decisions. Moreover, policy debates would have to be more generalized on the various levels of the organization so that recommendations to the management are carefully screened and debated from different angles.

The present transitional organization places the professional staff, on the basis of training, into economics, engineering, finance, and legal departments. Each department has junior and senior professional staff members, Kuwaitis and non-Kuwaitis. In addition, there is a research department staffed by several senior economists. Departments do not have department heads.

Instead, the administration of the fund consists of the director general, his deputy, and directors of administration, finance, operations, and research. All directors are Kuwaitis. It is obvious that the directors were not appointed to head the departments previously mentioned. The engineering, economics, and legal departments do not have directors, but the three departments (involved in what could be termed operations) are headed by the director of operations.

In actuality, however, the situation is more flexible and fluid than it would appear from a conventional organizational viewpoint. The decision-making arrangements continue to reflect a flexible task-oriented approach. The various directors do not have a specified set of formal responsibilities over their respective fields of activities and the professional staff working in those fields. The process of decision-making and the categorization of the decision structure offer an interesting case of centralization. The major decision center is the director general. However, one finds a flexible relationship between the management and the professional staff in terms of contributions to decisions. The management uses a collegial strategy to reach decisions involving professional evaluation of projects and loan applications or any other matter in which technical considerations arise. Such matters are discussed in meetings where everyone can give his opinion and will be able to argue for it. Management participates as an equal in a final process of voting, and the decision would reflect collective expertise more than the single opinion of the formal decision maker.

Although it is unrealistic to assume a total value consensus among all the people working in the fund, with regard to development goals and preferred societal targets at which the fund's policies and operations should aim, it is reasonable to assume a high degree of value consensus in regard to the professional targets in the fund's work. Such value consensus is assured through a delicate process of recruitment and by eschewing debates on ideological attitudes. The organizational structure most efficient in handling technical decisions based on majority judgment operates according to rules which

(1) require fidelity to the group's preference hierarchy; (2) require all members to participate in each decision; (3) route pertinent information about causation to each member; (4) give each member equal influence over the final choices; (5) designate as ultimate choice that alternative favored by the largest group of judges – the majority.(11)

These requirements seem to exist in the fund's decision structure for arriving at its routine technical decisions. That the management of the fund offers ample opportunity for the application of rule No. (4) is significant in relation to the overall effectiveness of the fund's operations. Adherence to this rule is important in maintaining the fund's image as a respected professional institution among regional and international development agencies.

POLICIES AND OPERATIONS

As mentioned earlier, the Kuwait Fund represents an organizational innovation for a national agency for foreign assistance. The policies and operations of the fund for the first decade indicate a cautious approach to development lending, leaning toward a conservative view of financial soundness. In this respect, the fund was principally influenced by the World Bank mode of operation. For the first crucial years of the fund's work, a legal adviser from the World Bank helped the fund develop policies and procedures for development lending.

Through the years, the fund management and staff acquired experience and confidence that helped the fund to sustain a good image among development financial institutions on both regional and international levels. The accumulated experience of the fund in the fields of development lending and the availability of highly qualified experts among the professional staff distinguish the fund's work among other development financing agencies. The contribution of the Kuwait Fund to Arab regional development cannot be measured only in terms of the amounts of loans given or the terms and conditions of such loans. The fund's contributions to Arab economic development in areas other than typical project financing are also important.

As a Kuwaiti institution, the fund performs an important function as adviser to the Kuwait government on various aspects of development services. The government called upon the fund for technical advice on establishing an industrial development bank in Kuwait. Arab experts working in the fund are called upon by Kuwait and other Arab countries for technical advice in establishing Arab and international investment institutions and related legal, economic, and financial issues.

In some instances, the fund has negotiated reciprocal trade agreements between Kuwait and other Arab countries. For example, it acted as an intermediary between Kuwait and the Sudan in an agreement under which the former was to supply the latter with fertilizer in exchange for livestock.(12) The Kuwait Fund also played an intermediary role between Algeria and its potential suppliers of funds by supporting an Algerian bond issue. This mediation role grew in importance when the fund helped Bahrain gain access to the World Bank and the International Monetary Fund. By helping Bahrain in its international diplomatic efforts, the fund enhanced the image of Kuwait as a leading state in the Arab Gulf area.(13)

The Kuwait Fund is occasionally approached by Arab countries to give advice on technical matters such as the establishment of national development banks. The fund helped establish a tourist and industrial development bank in Lebanon; the fund's research department conducted a survey of existing industrial development banks(14) and produced a well-defined scheme for a tourism and industrial development bank, which was presented to the Lebanese government.

The most important initiative of the Kuwait Fund, however, was on the collective level of Arab regional cooperation. The Kuwait Fund was a major force behind establishing two important financial regional institutions: The Arab Fund for Economic and Social Development, and the Inter-Arab Investment Guarantee Corporation.

On a proposal and preliminary draft submitted by the fund, the Kuwait government first suggested, at a conference of Arab finance ministers in Baghdad, in August 1967, the establishment of the Arab Fund. The final agreement that the Arab governments adopted in May 1968, however, was different from the draft presented by the Kuwait Fund. The 1968 agreement establishing the Arab Fund reflects the thinking of the Economic Council of the Arab League in the mid-1950s, which, in 1957, had proposed an Arab Financial Corporation. The articles of this 1957 proposal were very much influenced by the World Bank Articles of Agreement.(15)

The Inter-Arab Investment Guarantee Corporation is another significant initiative of the fund on the regional level. The fund's contribution in promoting a scheme for guaranteeing Arab investments in the Arab countries is in compliance with Kuwait's policy to encourage Kuwait's private investments in the Arab region.

The fund first proposed three complementary agreements deemed necessary to encourage inter-Arab investments. The first concerned objective rules of investment (for example, how Arab investments should be treated by the recipient country in terms of taxation on profits to the investor's country). The second concerned methods of settling disputes that arise in the investment process by stipulating procedures for conciliation and arbitration of such disputes. The third concerned a program for guaranteeing the investments, which the investor might consider as a last resort when he feels that his investment is not well enough protected by the first two agreements.

Later on, the fund realized the difficulties that might arise if the three agreements were linked in one document. Some of the Arab countries might find the stipulations of the first and second agreements inappropriate for them to abide by, despite their interest in and acceptance of the rules for guaranteeing investments made in their countries.

In order to get a consensus of the Arab governments, the final draft of the articles of the agreement for establishing the corporation included only rules pertaining to the guarantee of investments. The purpose of the finally adopted document of the Inter-Arab Investment Guarantee Corporation is to cover the Arab investor against

> the risk of expropriation, nationalization, sequestration and other similar measures which deprive the investor of substantial rights over his property; the risk for the investor of being unable to transfer his income, capital amortization installments or debt repayments out of the host country as a result of additional exchange control restrictions; and lastly, the risk of material damage due to war, military operations, insurrections, civil disturbances, etc.(16)

The agreement establishing the Inter-Arab Investment Corporation became effective when twelve Arab countries ratified it. The first meeting of the board of directors of the corporation took place in Kuwait in 1974.

The Kuwait Fund has, more recently, played an important role in bringing about two important aid institutions: the Arab Bank for Economic Development in Africa and the OPEC Special Fund. Experts from the Kuwait Fund helped in the technical preparatory stage of discussions and negotiations that culminated in the establishment of the two institutions. A senior legal adviser from the Kuwait Fund, who participated in the technical design of the OPEC Fund, later became its director general.

The discussion above of the Kuwait Fund contributions to Arab development covers areas other than project lending and financing. Below we deal with the various aspects of the fund's lending activities by discussing the politics of the fund operations, the project and policy process, and the development strategy of the fund.

The Politics of the Kuwait Fund

The Kuwait Fund was established immediately after Kuwait acquired independence, with the purpose of strengthening Kuwait's newly acquired sovereign status among the Arab countries in particular and the rest of the world in general. In this vein, the establishment of the fund was a political decision and the purposes of the fund were ultimately political. However, the administration of the fund is not as strongly politicized as in the case of the Abu Dhabi Fund.(17) The political aspects of the Kuwait Fund are more subtle; this is evident in the degree to which political considerations are not obvious in decisions on loans and technical assistance, and the degree of independence that the fund management enjoys in making decisions.

Table 1.1 shows Kuwait Fund loans by country and project until mid-1977, Table 1.2 shows the amount of technical assistance through 1976, and Table 1.3 shows sectoral and geographical distribution of loans for the same period. Egypt and the Sudan head the list of recipient countries in amounts of loans. Such recipients as the Arab Republic of Yemen and the People's Democratic Republic of Yemen receive relatively small amounts of the total loans, but almost half of the total amounts to each of the two countries are in interest-free loans. The distribution of loans among the rest of the countries reflects a balanced picture. (Lebanon is a special case, because of constant civil disturbances since 1975.) It is difficult to detect a political pattern of lending in the Kuwait Fund. The strong emphasis on Egypt could be interpreted as a form of support for Egypt's Arab and foreign policies that followed the October 1973 war. However, the same emphasis on Egypt could be explained in terms of the real needs of the Egyptian economy for hard currencies and the vast investment opportunities and high absorptive capacity of that economy. Sudan has traditionally received the fund's attention, reflecting the acute capital shortage in that country. A search for political considerations in the fund's lending would be a hair-splitting exercise, since no obvious pattern emerges.(18)

There is evidence that the fund management has a high degree of independence in making its lending decisions.(19) Direct interference by the ministry of foreign affairs in the early years of the fund's operations, if it existed, was vigorously rejected by the fund management. It has been noted that the remarkable degree of independence the Kuwait Fund enjoys can be attributed to the special nature of Kuwait's political society and the efforts of the fund's director general.(20)

Indeed, the fund enjoys a high degree of independence, but it should be remembered that the fund's enabling law makes the board of directors, and specifically the chairman, responsible for the fund's policies. This political overseeing is of greater significance to the government, in view of the fund's expanded scope of operations and drastically increased capital. The ultimate political control of the fund by the government leaves no doubt as to its political nature, but at the same time it explains the degree of independence

TABLE 1.1. PROJECT LOANS OF THE KUWAIT FUND FOR ARAB ECONOMIC DEVELOPMENT (until June 19, 1977)

Project	Country	Amount KD* (in millions)	Date	Lending Conditions % **	Maturity	Grace Period Yr./Mo.
Sudan railways	Sudan	7.0	3/1962	4	15.7	3.7
Yarmouk Valley project	Jordan	1.89	4/1962	3	20	5.0
Phosphate mines	Jordan	2.99	4/1962	4	10	3.5
Jerusalem electricity	Jordan	.24	2/1964	3	17.02	1.2
Jerusalem Hotel	Jordan	.18	2/1964	4	11.7	1.7
Jordan Hotel	Jordan	.08	3/1965	3.5	24.2	0.6
La Goulette electricity, Phase 1	Tunisia	3.80	12/1963	4	15.5	3.5
Medjerda Valley (1)	Tunisia	2.00	12/1963	3	14.6	4.4
Oil pipeline, Phase 1	Algeria	7.5	6/1964	4	14.7	2.7
Suez Canal expansion	Egypt	9.80	7/1964	4	16	3.0
Sugar plant	Sudan	1.67	7/1965	4	14.4	2.4
Tessaout agricultural project	Morocco	7.35	5/1966	3	24	4.0
Tadla agricultural project	Morocco	2.70	5/1966	3	19	4.0
Joun electricity	Lebanon	1.66	7/1966	4	12.5	2.5
La Goulette electricity project, Phase 2	Tunisia	4.55	1/1967	4	14.6	2.6

* 1 KD = $3.47 (recent exchange rate)
** including 0.5% Administrative Charges

(Table 1.1 Continued)

Project	Country	Amount KD* (in millions)	Date	Lending Conditions % **	Maturity	Grace Period Yr./Mo.
Oil pipeline Phases 2 and 3	Algeria	2.5	5/1967	4	11.8	0.0
Agricultural development	Sudan	4.21	8/1967	3	21.3	2.8
Cargo ships construction	Egypt	3.50	1/1968	4	14.9	2.9
Wadi Zabid project	Yemen	.33	6/1968	0.5	47	9.0
Grain silos	Lebanon	.80	8/1968	4	11.4	2.4
Grain silos	Syria	7.00	8/1969	3.5	15.5	3.5
Aluminum smelter	Bahrain	.99	7/1970	4	11.9	1.9
Medjerda Valley (2)	Tunisia	3.20	7/1970	3	26.4	6.4
Salif salt mine	Yemen	3.00	7/1970	2	19	2.0
Samarrah hydro-electric project	Iraq	2.63	12/1970	4	14.5	2.5
Gas pipeline	Tunisia	.90	2/1971			
Flour mill	Bahrain	.50	3/1971	4	11.7	1.7
Causeway and bridge	Bahrain	.50	3/1971	3	14.2	0.2
Agricultural survey and Wadi Abyan development studies	South Yemen	.33	4/1971	0.5	49.1	9.1
Samawah/UM Qasr cement project	Iraq	3.76	8/1971	4	13.1	2.1
Sucrafor project	Morocco	.85	2/1972	4	9.7	1.7
Mechanized dry farming	Sudan	1.60	3/1972	3	24.2	4.2
Zarqa River project	Jordan	4.6	3/1972	3	24.5	4.5

(Table 1.1 Continued)

Project	Country	Amount KD* (in millions	Date	% **	Maturity	Lending Conditions Grace Period Yr./Mo.
Sitra power-water causeway	Bahrain	7.35	7/1972	4	18	3.4
Highway project	Yemen	.28	8/1972	0.5	49	9.4
Rahad irrigation	Sudan	3.30	4/1973	3	30	4.5
Tihama development project	Yemen	1.90	6/1973	0.5	50	10.1
Hussein thermal power project	Jordan	3.02	6/1973	4	24	4
Abu Qier gas field development	Egypt	4.5	7/1973	4	20	5
Northwest Sennar sugar project	Sudan	4.5	7/1973	4	16	4
Petroleum refinery	Syria	2.00	3/1974	1	24	4.5
Suez Canal reopening	Egypt	10.00	3/1974	4	18	3
Fishing ports at Sfax, Chabba, and Zarziz	Tunisia	2.85	3/1974	3	19	4
Abyan delta project	South Yemen	4.20	5/1974	0.5	49	9.4
Talkha chemical fertilizer project	Egypt	7.00	6/1974	4	20	4.1
Industrial development Bank of Jordan	Jordan	1.00	7/1974	4	17	5
Phosphate mines development project	Tunisia	2.00	10/1974	4	15	2.9
Meherda power plant	Syria	9.90	11/1974	4	19	2.7
Phosphoric acid and mono-ammonium phosphate project	Morocco	2.40	11/1974	4	14	3.7

(Table 1.1 Continued)

Project	Country	Amount KD* (in millions)	Date	% **	Lending Conditions	
					Maturity	Grace Period Yr./Mo.
National Bank, Economic Devel.	Tunisia	2.50	4/1975	4	16	4.4
Highway maintenance	Mauritania	1.15	4/1975	0.5	25	4.7
Mukalla-Hadramout highway	South Yemen	4.50	6/1975	1.5	25	9.2
Tea plantation	Rwanda	1.00	6/1975	3	27	6.6
Palong land settlement	Malaysia	7.60	6/1975	5	30	10.4
Rahad irrigation (2)	Sudan	11.20	6/1975	3	31	5.5
Industrial Bank	Sudan	1.50	6/1975	4	16	4
Livestock devel.	Uganda	5.75	6/1975	2.5	25	4.5
Rural electrification	Bangladesh	6.40	6/1975	2	32	6.8
Manu River	Bangladesh	2.30	6/1975	1.5	33	7.5
Textile plant	Tanzania	4.50	7/1975	4	22	4.6
Abu Qier gas (2)	Egypt	3.50	7/1975	4	20	5
Mogadiscio power	Somalia	6.20	7/1975	1.5	29.1	4.1
National Development Bank	Morocco	6.00	8/1975	7	15.3	3.3
Quneitra electricity	Morocco	3.50	9/1975	4	17.5	3.5
Urea plant	Sri Lanka	7.50	9/1975	4	19	4.1
Carthage airport	Tunisia	4.00	10/1975	4	20	4.4
Abu Qier power	Egypt	10.00	10/1975	4	20	5
Nouakchott-Kiffa road	Mauritania	8.80	10/1975	0.5	25	4.9

(Table 1.1 Continued)

Project	Country	Amount KD* (in millions)	Date	Lending Conditions		
				% **	Maturity	Grace Period Yr./Mo.
Kulekhani hydro-electric	Nepal	5.00	1/1976	3	31.6	6.6
Taiz-KM 64 highway	Yemen	1.50	1/1976	1.5	39	9.1
Tihama Devel. (2)	Yemen	2.80	1/1976	0.5	47.5	7.5
Kalinadi hydro-electric project	India	15.00	1/1976	4	25	5
Nouadibou port	Mauritania	2.45	2/1976	1.5	25	5
Tunis-Turki road	Tunis	3.75	2/1976	4	20	5
Benzert bridge	Tunis	2.25	2/1976	4	20	5
Guddu-Karachi transmission line	Pakistan	13.00	N.A.	4	20	5
Electric projects in three constituencies	Thailand	1.00	1976	3.5	25	5
Jordan Industrial Bank	Jordan	2.50	1976	3.5	16.5	4
Telephone communication (stage 1)	Guinea	2.70	1976	4.0	17	3
Main roads	Comoros	1.80	1976	1	40	10
Fertilizer project	Egypt	3.20	1976	4.0	20	3
North Somal project	Somalia	6.00	1976	1	39	8
Airport extension	Maldives	1.50	1976	1	20	6
Coffee plantation	Burundi	.36	1976	3.0	26	7
Fertilizer project (No. 2)	Egypt	3.20	1976	N.A.	N.A.	N.A.
S. Dam	Mali	5.00	1976	2.5	26	6

(Table 1.1 Continued)

Project	Country	Amount KD* (in millions)	Date	Lending Conditions % **	Maturity	Grace Period Yr./Mo.
Phosphate project	Jordan	7.13	1976	4.0	14	1.9
Livestock project	Senegal	1.20	1976	3.0	26	5
Feasibility studies	Sudan	.90	8/1976	1.5	39	9
Natural gas pipelines	Oman	7.50	11/1976	4.0	20	N.A.
Al-Mukalla multipurpose	South Yemen	2.70	11/1976	3.0	17	2.0
Railway modernization	Congo	4.00	12/1976	4.0	17	3.7
Hydroelectric power plant (Song Loulou)	Cameroon	4.50	2/1977	4.0	25	5
Ras-Shukair oil pipeline	Egypt	7.00	2/1977	4.0	17	3.6
Zamboanga electrification	Philippines	3.50	3/1977	4.0	19	3.4
Qued El-Makhazine dam	Morocco	10.00	3/1977	3.0	25	5.5
Bandung electricity distribution	Indonesia	8.80	4/1977	4.0	20	5.1
Highway	Madagascar	2.10	4/1977	4.0	16	3.6
Livestock devel.	Yemen	3.50	4/1977	2.0	34	9.2
Kpong hydro-electric	Ghana	8.97	4/1977	4.0	20	5.0
Sennar-Damazin highway	Sudan	9.00	6/1977	3.0	20	5.3
Railway	Pakistan	7.30	6/1977	4.0	18	3
Baghland sugar factory	Afghanistan	8.85	6/1977	3.5	23	4

(Table 1.1 Continued)

Project	Country	Amount KD* (in millions)	Date	Lending Conditions % **	Maturity	Grace Period Yr./Mo.
Nicosia-Limassol road	Cyprus	1.13	6/1977	5.0	15	3.2
Tringano palm oil	Malaysia	2.30	6/1977	5.0	23	6.8
Phosphate production expansion	Jordan	8.90	6/1977	4.0	15	2.8
TOTAL		441.00				

Source: The Permanent Mission of the State of Kuwait to the United Nations, Press Release No. 2/77 (11 October 1977).

TABLE 1.2. KUWAIT FUND TECHNICAL ASSISTANCE
(until end of 1976)

Project	Country	Date	Amount KD
Farah Ruh; sugar factory	Afghanistan	11/74	400,000
Livestock study	Afghanistan		33,000
Technical assistance team- power supply	Bahrain		100,000
Technical assistance	Chad		230,000
Road	Guinea	7/75	150,000
Bissau port and airport	Guinea-Bissau	7/75	200,000
Arab Planning Institute		1970-75	89,173
Cement and agricultural development	Mali	6/75	200,000
Mineral wealth	Mauritania	2/75	175,000
Dairy project	Nepal	6/75	90,000
Livestock development; irrigated agricultural project	Somalia	2/75	200,000
Sennar sugar factory; grain storage	Sudan	3/72	100,000
Transportation study	Sudan	4/73	300,000
Technical assistance team	Yemen	7/71	71,429
Technical assistance team, Phase 2	Yemen	9/73	100,000
Bajil textile factory	Yemen	9/71	25,000
Geological survey	Yemen	4/72	85,000
Tihama development	Yemen	7/72	50,000
Livestock wealth	Yemen	2/74	80,000
Increased cement production	Yemen	1/75	70,000
Technical assistance team, Phase 3	Yemen	6/75	125,000

(Table 1.2 Continued)

Project	Country	Date	Amount KD
Fish meal; fish oil	South Yemen	7/72	100,000
Aden, Rayan ports; livestock development	South Yemen	6/74	300,000
Technical assistance planning, statistics	South Yemen		110,000
Sugar industry; hydro power	Uganda	6/75	230,000
Economic Commission for West Asia		6/75	50,000
Fishing port	Senegal	9/75	200,000
Oil and soap project	Mali	1976	200,000
Fishing development	Maldives	1976	100,000
Experts	Comoros	1976	100,000
Fish resources development	Mauritania	12/76	150,000
Livestock development	Oman	12/76	150,000
Technical staff for Industrial Bank	Yemen Arab Rep.	11/76	125,000
Grain silos	Southern Yemen	11/76	7,500
Training program, economic planning	Arab Planning Institute	11/76	50,000
Transportation system development	Gambia	12/76	300,000
Sugar plantation development	Vietnam	12/76	150,000
Dubreka-Boke road (Stage 2)	Guinea	3/77	100,000
Agricultural Resources development	Bahrain	1/77	70,000
Fishing Resources development; Sewerage purification	Malta	3/77	70,000
TOTAL			5,486,102

Source: The Permanent Mission of the State of Kuwait to the United Nations, Press Release No. 2/77 (11 October 1977).

TABLE 1.3. SECTORAL AND GEOGRAPHICAL DISTRIBUTION
OF KUWAIT FUND LOANS TO ARAB COUNTRIES
(January 1, 1962–June 30, 1977)

Country	Agri-culture	Transport Commu-nications and Storage	Electri-city	Industry	Total KD (million)	%*
Algeria	10.000				10.000	3.3
Bahrain		0.500	7.350	1.490	9.340	3.1
Egypt		34.800	10.000	13.700	58.500	19.4
Iraq			2.620	3.760	6.380	2.1
Jordan	6.480		3.260	23.010	32.750	10.8
Lebanon		0.800	1.660		2.460	0.8
Mauritania		9.400			9.400	3.1
Morocco	20.050		3.500	9.250	32.800	10.9
Oman				7.500	7.500	2.5
Somalia	6.000		6.200		12.200	4.0
Sudan	20.310	16.000		8.570	44.880	14.9
Syria		7.000	9.900	2.000	18.900	6.3
Tunisia	5.200	13.750	8.350	4.500	31.800	10.5
Northern Yemen	8.520	1.780		3.000	13.300	4.4
Southern Yemen	4.530	4.500		2.700	11.730	3.9
TOTAL	71.090	98.530	52.840	79.480	301.940	100.0
%*	23.5	32.6	17.5	26.3	100.0	

*Percentages may not add up to 100 because of rounding

Source: The Kuwait Fund for Arab Economic Development, Annual Report 1976–1977. p. 102

the fund management has over its operations. Since critical policies and decisions can be checked by the chairman of the board, there is no need for interference in the fund's operations by other organs of the government.

The absence of direct interference in the fund's operations has helped the fund to maintain a commitment to high standards of professional performance. There is a definite attempt to adhere to sound procedures in investigating loan applications and in appraising development projects. The ability of the fund to project the image of a highly professional institution has worked favorably from a political viewpoint. Kuwait has found that it pays politically if the fund maintains a strong and solid professional image that is not colored by political leanings. An observer noted in 1973, "Although the Fund has given in project loans less than half the amount given by the Kuwait government in 'political' loans, there is growing recognition that the Fund's money has been more effectively spent, even from the point of view of political prestige."(21)

The Project and Policy Process

As indicated earlier, the fund started its project lending operations with expert advice from the World Bank. As the fund gained more experience, its work reflected the particular circumstances of the Arab world. This is more obvious in areas of technical assistance and extra lending activities, as discussed earlier. The fund's work in such fields was distinguished by an active approach in extending technical services to Kuwait and other Arab countries in economic development and particularly development financing. In project work, the fund is still influenced by the policies the World Bank used to follow in the late fifties and early sixties. As a matter of policy, the fund refrains from involvement in educational development, health, or population projects.

The recently enacted fund charter stipulates some principles to be observed in considering loan applications and in concluding loan agreements. These stipulations portray the fund's effort to evolve its practices along guidelines derived from its experience in the region, and to reflect its image as an Arab lending institution.

Article 20 of the fund's charter states that in considering loan applications the fund shall be guided by the recognized principles of development finance, particularly the following:

1. the degree of importance of the project or program for which the loan is requested and its priority in relation to other projects or programs;

2. the completeness and accuracy of the cost estimates for the project or program;

3. the adequacy of the economic technical evaluation of the project;

4. ascertainment of the availability of other funds necessary, in addition to fund financing, for the execution and completion of the project or program;

5. the solvency of the applicant or the guarantor.

Article 21 of the charter stipulates that all loan agreements between the fund and the borrowers are to be made in the Arabic language (although an increasing number of the borrowers are non-Arab). Article 18 stipulates that all loan agreements between the fund and the borrowers should include the following:

1. financial clauses specifying the duration allowed and conditions for withdrawal of proceeds of the loans, and the dates and conditions for the repayment of the principal thereof and payment of interest, if any, and other charges on the loan;

2. an undertaking by the borrower to furnish sufficient information to the fund on the progress of work on the project financed, starting from the date the loan agreement is signed until the loan is fully repaid;

3. an undertaking by the borrower to provide all the necessary facilities to enable fund representatives to follow up the progress of the project financed;

4. provisions for ensuring that the amounts withdrawn from the loan shall be used exclusively for financing expenditures on the project financed and only as such expenditures are actually incurred;

5. an undertaking that no other external debt shall have priority over the fund loan or the interest or other charges thereon by way of a lien on the assets of the borrower, except such limits as the fund may accept;

6. an undertaking to exempt all transactions, assets, and income of the fund in the recipient state from all taxes, dues, and other impositions;

7. an undertaking by the monetary or other competent authority in the recipient state to facilitate all the financial operations of the fund and, in particular, to lift all foreign exchange restrictions on direct and indirect transfers arising out of the loan agreement;

8. an undertaking to consider all fund documents, records, correspondence, and similar material, confidential and to accord the fund full immunity from censorship and inspection of printed matters;

9. an undertaking to exempt all the assets and income of the fund from nationalization, confiscation, and seizure.

Where the loan is made to an entity other than the state, the undertakings set out in 6, 7, 8 and 9 would be incorporated in a guarantee agreement to be concluded between the fund and the government of the state guaranteeing the loan.

Almost all of Kuwait Fund lending is in project loans. The fund has refrained from entering the area of program lending. In January 1974, the director general of the fund declared, "We simply do not have the resources necessary to underwrite, even in part, whole development programs in more than twelve recipient countries."(22) To emphasize the implausibility of program lending, he added, "When the biggest and the most experienced bilateral source of aid, the United States, declares that it will no longer have country programs, that it will prefer to react to recipient's initiatives, and that it intends to rely on international finance institutions to appraise the overall development prospects of a country, we should, I feel, be rather ill-advised to enter the ambitious program finance business, even if we had the resources to do so."(23) These statements were made before the enactment of Law 25 (1974) which raised the fund's capital to $3.55 billion and expanded its geographical domain of operations to include all developing countries.

The Kuwait Fund strongly favors project lending for many reasons. The fund has already built a considerable experience in project lending procedures and techniques. The composition of the fund's professional staff seems to be geared toward specific task-oriented appraisal techniques that characterize project lending. Program lending would entail development policy debates and would require more background work, in terms of preinvestment studies and preparations, than is required for project lending. With a limited number of qualified personnel available, a shift to program lending, which requires a larger staff and wider scope of specializations, would burden the fund. Moreover, project lending has some political advantages over program lending because it permits the lending agency to exercise a higher degree of control over the disbursement process. Such a high degree of control enables the fund to avoid misuse of its money by various groups in the borrowing country.

It is significant that the fund's new charter mentions both project and program loans in describing the fund's operations.(24) With the increase in its resources, the fund will be able to extend program loans if it chooses to do so.(25) Program loans have certain advantages from lender and recipient points of view. In terms of using aid as an incentive or a means for influencing self-help measures, program lending provides a more effective means of influencing broad governmental policies in the recipient country than does project lending.(26) Since program loans finance import require- ments for an economy as a whole, the borrowing country is usually more willing to accept conditions relating to its overall economic policies than it would if the loans were project-specific. This kind of leverage might be particularly useful if the fund decided to get involved in certain development programs geared toward specific objectives. Programs designed to promote economic integration among the Arab economies or those aimed at achieving self-sufficiency in food production for the Arab world are cases in point. Program lending in such instances would enable the fund to use its resources in a more innovative and effective way to promote regional development.

After the enactment of Law 25 (1974) the Kuwait Fund increased its volume of lending appreciably. During 1975 and 1976, the fund signed project loan agreements for about KD 186 million, as compared with KD 151 million for the previous 12 years. Such a large increase reflects a determined expansion in the fund's lending operations, which must tax the fund's financial and manpower resources. The challenge that faces the fund does not lie primarily in the financial aspects of lending, since paid-in capital can be increased accordingly, but in areas such as identification, selection, and supervision of projects.

The Kuwait Fund has an ad hoc policy in regard to identifying and selecting the projects it finances. The fund usually responds to the initiatives of borrowing countries, which present the fund with lists of projects to be financed. Such a process of identifying and selecting projects for financing suffers from the shortcomings associated with inadequate project preparations, which are prevalent in most developing countries.(27) Lending institutions such as the World Bank have tried to overcome such shortcomings by getting more actively involved in the project identification and selection process in the borrowing countries. To support such activities, the World Bank conducts regular economic surveys covering individual countries and sometimes regional groupings. Such an awesome undertaking is beyond the fund's present capabilities. However, as will be discussed in later chapters, the fund could cooperate with other development financing institutions in the region to improve tremendously the present process by which projects are identified and selected for external financing.

The fund's supervision of its projects is considered satisfactory. With the drastic increase in number of projects, however, such supervision would be more difficult to exercise. The professional staff recognizes this problem as a limiting factor in the fund's ability to expand its volume of lending in the future.

Development Strategy

Questions of development strategy do not constitute a major concern in the Kuwait Fund. In statements by fund management(28) and in discussions with research department senior members, there was no advocacy of a given development strategy for the fund to pursue in its lending operations. As Table 1.4 shows, the fund concentrates on infrastructure projects and industry.   It shuns financing social projects in education, health, or population. A recent departure, however, was the fund's support, by KD 7.6 million, for the Palong land settlement project in Malaysia. The objective of the loan is to help clear a forest area of 73,000 feddans, convert it into rubber plantations, and resettle about 5,500 families of poor landholders.(29)

The fund's loan costs range from interest-free loans (with only 0.5% service charge) to 5% interest, depending on the sector of the economy of the project and the economic conditions of the borrowing country, as shown in Table 1.1. Accordingly, the grant element in the fund's loans ranges between 25% for Phase II of the oil pipeline project in Algeria and 86% for the Abyan Delta project for the People's Democratic Republic of Yemen.

The fund research department has developed projects dealing with significant aspects of the fund's work, for which more research-based policy suggestions are needed. The fund plans two research projects on the process of project identification and on the appraisal of development projects. There are also plans to work on an inter-Arab investment code and on means to promote Arab industrial exports.

It is obvious to those working in the fund that their contributions toward a regional development strategy and measures to enhance economic integration opportunities in the Arab world are potentially the most significant achievement they can make. The Kuwait Fund management is well aware of the fund's opportunity to play a major role in Arab regional development strategy and the particular contributions of the fund to it are yet to be achieved.(31)

TABLE 1.4. SECTORAL DISTRIBUTION OF
KUWAIT FUND LOANS
(January 1962 – June 1977)

Sector	%
Agricultural	22.1
Transport, Communications, and Storage	27.4
Electricity	27.4
Industry	23.1
TOTAL	100.0

Source: The Kuwait Fund for Arab Economic Development, Annual Report 1976-1977, p. 101.

2 Abu Dhabi Fund For Arab Economic Development

The Abu Dhabi Fund was established in July 1971 with a declared capital of 50 million Bahraini dinars,(1) which is equivalent to U.S. $150 million.(2) It was inspired, to a great extent, by the model of the Kuwait Fund for Arab Economic Development, created ten years earlier. The main function of the Abu Dhabi Fund was to extend economic assistance to Arab countries "in the form of loans or participation in projects or guarantees or any other form that shall be defined by the regulations of the Fund."(3) The fund started operating in June 1972, and its board of directors first met in November that year.(4) After the substantial increase in oil revenues of Abu Dhabi in 1973, the authorized capital of the fund was increased in July 1974 to 2 billion UAE dirhams,(5) equivalent to U.S. $500 million.

In the next two sections we discuss the management of the fund and its policies and operations.

THE MANAGEMENT OF ABU DHABI FUND

Management of the Abu Dhabi Fund rests with the board of directors. As in similar organizations (e.g., the Kuwait Fund) the board of directors usually provides broad policy guidance and legitimization functions. The day-to-day activities are managed by a general manager and a limited group of senior experts. For a clearer picture of how the Abu Dhabi Fund is managed, we deal separately with the board of directors, the general manager, and the internal organization of the fund.

The Board of Directors

According to the Articles of Internal Regulations, issued in 1971 by the Emir of Abu Dhabi, the board of directors has the following functions:

1. Consider and take decisions concerning applications for loans, partici-

25

pation in projects, and other forms of assistance offered by the fund.

2. Decide on the forms of participation in projects in Arab states and countries.

3. Approve the amounts of loans, participation, and other forms of assistance.

4. Fix the conditions for participation in projects within the overall regulations set for the fund.

5. Determine channels for the investment of monies of the fund.

6. Fix the size and conditions of the capital raised by the fund.

7. Draw up staff regulations for the fund and supervise their implementation.

8. Approve the fund's annual budget and its financial statements.

The regulations stipulated that the board could delegate whatever it deemed suitable of its powers to the general manager of the fund. The regulations also stipulated that the board of directors "shall hold at least six meetings per year, called for by the chairman."

The functions of the board, as described in the fund's internal regulations, require the board to play an active policy role. Also, by detailing the requirements for the achievement of the fund's objectives in precise functional terms, the board is expected to convey a professional outlook in its work. The composition of the board, however, stresses political considerations that would leave little room for active professional policy involvement by the board of directors in the fund's work.

The board consists of seven members in addition to the general manager. It includes cabinet members, among whom are the minister of foreign affairs and the minister of oil and finance. The board is chaired by the prime minister. The general manager of the fund is a board member with no voting rights. The decisions of the board are made by a majority vote except in a few cases where a two-thirds majority is required.

The General Manager

The internal regulations of the fund, issued by the Emir in 1971, refer to the general manager as the person directly responsible for all administrative, financial, and technical matters in the fund.

The responsibilities of the general manager are detailed as follows:

1. Carry out the decisions of the board.

2. Prepare the draft budget of the fund and submit it to the board of directors.

3. Authorize expenditure in accordance with the budget allocations.

4. Receive and study applications for loans and economic assistance, and submit reports on such loans and economic assistance to the board of directors.

5. Implement loan contracts.

6. Execute tasks assigned to him by the board of directors.

The position of the general manager was left vacant when the fund was established in 1971. Hassan Abbas Zaki, a former Egyptian minister of economy, was appointed an adviser to the Abu Dhabi Fund. Dr. Zaki was assigned the tasks of laying out the ground rules for the organization and operation of the fund and developing working relationships between the fund and other financial institutions within and outside the Arab region. Dr. Zaki, who was economic adviser to the Emir (ruler of Abu Dhabi) at that time, was appointed a deputy chairman of the board of directors in 1972, with the powers of the general manager. He was later appointed general manager of the fund.*

In 1974 an United Nations Conference on Trade and Development (UNCTAD) consultant observed that the provisions for an active board of directors were not likely to materialize, "The early evidence suggests that the Board will not develop (as an active policymaking organ)" and added that "it seems likely, and desirable, that more informal and flexible relationships will be developed for determining the trust of Fund's operations."(6)

It seems the fund has found a workable arrangement that helps to provide continuity and smoothness of operation on the top managerial level. What has developed are regular monthly or biweekly meetings that include the minister of foreign affairs (a board member), the general manager, his deputy (who is an Abu Dhabi national), and a selected group of senior experts of the fund. Such meetings provide certain institutional advantages that reflect favorably on the work of the fund, as follows:

1. Professional considerations that are significant for the fund's work are discussed routinely and effectively. As indicated earlier, the high value that the fund's creators placed on political considerations was translated into the composition of the board of directors, so that important cabinet members are included.

2. Professional considerations are kept in perspective. Regular and routine meetings give an opportunity for various technical points of view to be presented and discussed. Although it is recognized that political considerations have played a prominent role since the fund started its work, there is also a cognizance that future development of the fund should result in assigning a greater weight to professional considerations in the fund's lending and technical assistance decisions.

---

*In March 1978, Mr. Nasser Al-Nowais was appointed general manager of the fund.

3. Regular meetings perform an informative function. The participants constitute a wide range of technical and political backgrounds. Hence, these meetings make possible the discussion of technical matters from varied viewpoints, leading to more reasoned decisions.

Internal Organizations

The Abu Dhabi Fund was unique among Arab national aid agencies in that its top managerial post was not held by a national of Abu Dhabi. In the Iraqui, Kuwaiti, and Saudi funds, the top managerial post is held by a national of the fund's home state. Recently, however, an Abu Dhabi national was appointed general manager. The organization chart for the Abu Dhabi Fund as of March 31, 1976, is shown in Fig. 2.1.

Five operational departments conduct the fund's day-to-day operations and handle the fund's main work as a lending agency. These are the projects, loan-implementation investment, accounting, and administrative departments. In addition, a research department engages mainly in information gathering and publication functions. The policy analysis and advisory functions rest with the experts, who report directly to the general manager and his deputy.

The present organizational structure raises some issues that are bound to have an influence on the overall effectiveness of the fund. The staffing of the operational departments indicates an imbalance in the distribution of the limited expertise available.

The projects department has three economists, three financial analysts, and one engineer. The director holds a Ph.D. in economics. This department handles the principal work load of the fund in terms of lending and technical assistance. The staff of the projects department, especially its director, are overworked in view of the tasks they are expected to handle. Such a situation usually creates either delays in handling the tasks or a deterioration in work quality. Supervision of projects to which loans are extended also rests with the projects department. This function has not made a major demand on the fund's staff time as yet, because of the slow rate of disbursement in relation to total commitments, but may rightfully belong to the next department discussed.

The loan-implementation department is more of a service department than an actual operations department. It has two staff members: an accountant and another staff member with private banking experience. The department handles routine questions on procurement rather than project management.(7)

The investment department manages the fund's portfolio. Major investment decisions, however, are made on a higher level since the department is not headed by a senior staff member. The department's five staff members include an accountant.

The research department is larger than the others except for the projects department. It is headed by an able economist, assisted by nine junior staff members. The work of the research department is not directly geared toward operations. Rather, it revolves generally around problems of economic development and particularly on issues of oil, energy, and recent develop-

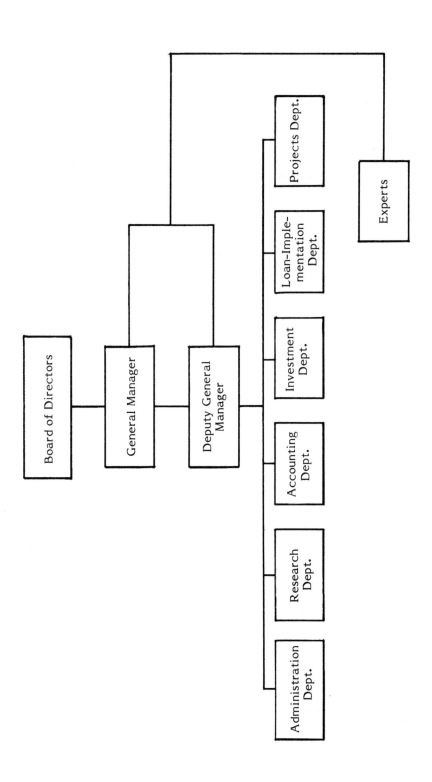

FIG. 2.1. ORGANIZATION CHART OF ABU DHABI FUND as of March 31, 1976

ments in international monetary and economic circles. The department issues a monthly bulletin, in English, that surveys developments in the world economy and summarizes news gathered from periodicals and publications of international economic organizations. The research department occasionally produces papers on issues of interest to Abu Dhabi as an Arab oil producer.

The accounting department (four accountants) and the administration department (seven staff members) offer the support services connected with internal auditing and personnel administration. The administration department is not involved in operations and does not appraise projects for which the management structure needs to be evaluated.

The present distribution of staff in the various departments shows an imbalance. Although the projects department has the largest staff, and probably the more qualified members, the department is relatively under-staffed in view of the workload it handles. This is also apparent in the loan-implementation department which, if properly staffed, would render a much needed service in a development lending agency (viz., the follow-up and supervision of project implementation and management). The specializations and qualifications of the professional staff of the Abu Dhabi Fund are shown in Table 2.1

TABLE 2.1. PROFESSIONAL STAFF OF ABU DHABI FUND
AS OF MARCH 31, 1976

Specialization	Educational Level			Total
	Ph.D.	M.A.	B.A.	
Economists	4	–	2	6
Financial analysts	1	–	3	4
Legal experts	1	1	–	2
Engineers	–	1	1	2
Accountants	–	1	5	6
Banking experts	–	–	5	5
Research assistants	–	1	8	9
TOTALS	6	4	24	34

Many of the highly qualified members of the professional staff are not assigned to the operational departments. As shown in the organization chart (Fig. 2.1), the experts group, not part of the operational departments organizationally, works in an advisory capacity and reports directly to the general manager and his deputy.

The experts group includes three economists, one financial analyst, two legal experts, and one engineer. Most of them are professionals with long work experience and advanced academic degrees. Their contributions to the work of the fund cannot easily be determined. Because of organizational sensitivity (in terms of lines of command), these professionals are not asked directly by the operational department heads to make intensive contributions to decisions on ongoing work. At the same time, since the projects department handles the bulk of the fund's work, there is usually a flow of communications between the director of that department and the various experts. Such communications regarding the contribution of experts to operational decisions sometimes need to be channeled through the general manager or his deputy to offer the proper organizational context for the experts' contribution. This arrangement may not be the most effective. The fund obviously suffers from a shortage of highly qualified technical experts, and the few that the fund has are not kept in the mainstream of the fund's operational work. Rather, they are treated as advisers outside of the organizational lines of the operations departments. It is suggested that a reorganization that would integrate the experts in the mainstream of the organizational structure of the operations departments is both workable and desirable. Such an integration would bolster the present operations departments and raise the effectiveness of the fund's work. We presume that such integration may result in some personal sensitivities in the first period of a reorganization. However, this may be more than compensated for in terms of the prospective increase in the fund's effectiveness and the enhancement of its professional image among development lending agencies in the region.

The decision-making arrangements in the Abu Dhabi Fund are not clear. One reason is the lack of integration of the expert group into the day-to-day operational activities. The most prominent figure in the decision-making process is the general manager, who also served as economic adviser to the ruler of Abu Dhabi. He is highly trusted by the political decision-makers, therefore offering a link needed between the political and professional tiers in decision-making. An important development in decision-making was introduced when the position of a deputy general manager was created and an Abu Dhabi national assumed the job. It is recognized that more managerial functions will be handled by the Abu Dhabi nationals in the fund. This could result later in a decrease in the degree of politicization of the board of directors and a movement toward a more professional outlook in the composition of the board. Such a movement would reflect the interests of the burgeoning business community in Abu Dhabi and the need to gear the Abu Dhabi Fund toward the service of better defined regional economic and business interests in the Gulf area in particular and in the Arab region in general.

Since the project department handles the major part of the day-to-day operations of the fund, its director, who joined the fund at its inception, plays a significant role in the decision-making process. He is more familiar with the developments that took place in the fund than most of the professional staff who joined the fund later. His professional competence and detailed knowledge of the fund's operations enable him to play an important role in bringing the contribution of the experts group into the day-to-day operations of the fund. Maintaining smooth working relationships between the rather detached experts group and the operational departments of the fund depends, indeed, on the ability of those involved to develop and maintain good interpersonal relations.

POLICIES AND OPERATIONS

The Law establishing the Abu Dhabi Fund, and the consequent regulations issued by the Emir of Abu Dhabi, gave the fund management, represented in its board of directors, complete freedom to determine the forms of assistance to be undertaken for achieving the fund's goals. Article 10, issued by the ruler of Abu Dhabi, indicated that the fund shall participate in Arab projects in the form of loans, participations, guarantees, or any other form prescribed by the board.

As indicated before, the Kuwait Fund, as a matter of policy, does not involve itself in equity participation, which the Abu Dhabi Fund has undertaken in some instances. In the case of Abu Dhabi Fund, equity participation is stipulated in the regulations as one form of assistance to be undertaken in fulfilling the fund's goal of extending economic assistance to the Arab countries. Thus, project participation is a distinguishing factor between the Kuwait and Abu Dhabi Funds.

There are not many conditions that the Abu Dhabi Fund is required to meet in its operations, except for the following:

1. The fund's contribution to any single project should not exceed 10% of the fund's capital.

2. The fund's contribution to any single project should not exceed 50% of the total cost of the project.

3. The project to which the fund is giving assistance should not be in conflict with the economic interests of Abu Dhabi or any other Arab country.

The first two conditions are intended to safeguard the fund's financial soundness. They can be waived, however, if a two-thirds majority of board members attending decide to do so in relation to a certain project. The third condition is intended as a political reminder that the fund's policies and operations should be in the interest of the Arab region in general and that of the donor country (Abu Dhabi) in particular. This condition could also be interpreted as an attempt by the fund to reduce the possibility of wasteful industrial duplication and to promote a semblance of a regional development strategy by inducing the borrower to operate within the framework of the area.(8)

By the end of 1976, the fund had signed agreements for project loans and equity participations totaling 1076.8 million UAE durham (or DH). A detailed description of these loans is given in Table 2.2.

In the following sections, we deal with politics in the fund's operations, the project and policy process in the fund, and whether a development strategy can be discerned in the fund's operations.

TABLE 2.2. LOANS AND EQUITY PARTICIPATION IN PROJECTS BY
ABU DHABI FUND FOR ARAB ECONOMIC DEVELOPMENT – 1974-1976
(UAE DH = $ 0.253)

Country	1974 Project Title	Loan Amt.	1975 Project Title	Loan Amt.	1976 Project Title	Loan Amt.	Total Loan Agreements (74-76) by Country	% of Country Loans to Total
Bahrain	Water and electricity	40.0			Small-scale industries. Sitra power and water station, stage 2	60.0 100.0	200.0	8.68
Bangla-desh					Completion and extension, machine-tools factory	40.0	40.0	3.74
Burundi					Fisheries development	4.0	4.0	0.37
Egypt	Talkha's second fertilizer factory	40.0	Electric power plant	130.0	Talkha urea plant, loan increase	18.4	206.4	9.28
	Constr. Omar Al Khayam Hotel I	10.0	Omar Khayam Hotel II	8.0				
India					Hydro power station	68.0	68.0	6.35

(Table 2.2 Continued)

Country	1974 Project Title	Loan Amt.	1975 Project Title	Loan Amt.	1976 Project Title	Loan Amt.	Total Loan Agreements (74-76) by Country	% of Country Loans to Total
Jordan	King Talal's Dam	21.5	Al-Azrak Al Hodoud Road	5.0			26.5	2.47
Malaysia					Sabah flour and F.M. Suai Oil Palm Project	16.0 17.0	33.0	3.08
Maldive					Freezing, storage ships, collec. boats	8.0	8.0	0.75
Mali					Silingue Dam	16.0	16.0	1.49
Morocco					Business center 2 cotton sp. mills	40.0 70.0	110.0	10.27
Oman					Exploit. transport. of natural gas	60.0	60.0	5.60
Sri Lanka					Fisheries develop.	20.0	20.0	1.87
Sudan					Cotton spinning m. Rural dev. S. Darfur	80.0 16.5	96.5	9.01

(Table 2.2 Continued)

Country	1974 Project Title	Loan Amt.	1975 Project Title	Loan Amt.	1976 Project Title	Loan Amt.	Total Loan Agreements (74-76) by Country	% of Country Loans to Total
Syria	Electrical dispatching center	51.5					51.5	4.81
Tunisia	Railway passenger cars Northern Sousa Land, and Tourism Project Metal cans project	13.5 31.7 6.0					57.2	4.78
Yemen A.R.	Can factory Sanaa's water	6.0 4.0	Rural Develop., Southern Uplands	40.0			44.0	4.11
Yemen D.R.					Fishing trawlers Geological survey, stage 1	29.1 6.6	35.7	3.33
Total		218.2		183.0		669.6	1076.8	100.00

Source: Hassan M. Selim, "Aid Process: The Experience of Abu Dhabi Fund for Arab Ecoomic Development." Paper submitted to UNCTAD meeting on Bilateral and Multilateral Financial and Technical Assistance Institutions. Geneva, March 14-22, 1977, pp. 5-6.

The Politics of the Abu Dhabi Fund

The organization and management aspects of the Abu Dhabi Fund reveal the weight given to political considerations. This is evident in the composition of the board of directors, in which the majority are cabinet members, including the minister of foreign affairs. The fund, however, is not the only source of foreign aid. It is noted that governments seeking economic aid from Abu Dhabi prefer to get it through channels other than the Abu Dhabi Fund (e.g., the foreign ministry or the ministry of finance). Although the fund's aid entails project examination and loan negotiations, and loans usually carry an interest rate of 5%, direct aid from the government of Abu Dhabi has more favorable conditions to the borrower (or grantee in many cases).(9) Any observer of the economic aid of the government of Abu Dhabi may conclude that such aid is highly political; this also may be true of the incipient operations of the Abu Dhabi Fund. This image, however, is changing and, especially in the case of the fund, the professional staff strongly feels that political considerations should exert less influence on the fund's operations than in the past. Technical considerations are assuming greater importance in the fund's decisions, because they present clear yardsticks for evaluating the projects. Consequently these considerations make decisions easier to reach. Policy makers in Abu Dhabi, and particularly those involved in the fund's decisions, realize that giving professionals in the fund the freedom to reach decisions on the basis of technical considerations presents some advantages to the policy makers: 1) it relieves them from time-consuming and sometimes embarrassingly long discussions with representatives of governments seeking aid. 2) The decisions reached are easily defended on the basis of professional expertise and technical criteria that are not easily challenged. 3) The image of the Abu Dhabi Fund as a professional organization would facilitate and encourage cooperation between the fund and the highly esteemed development lending institutions in the region and on the international level.

The increasing importance given to technical considerations in the fund's work is directly linked to cooperation between the fund and other development financing agencies, especially the Kuwait Fund and the Arab Fund. There is a mutual reinforcement mechanism between the two processes: the professionalization of the Abu Dhabi Fund work (meaning more reliance on technical considerations for reaching decisions), and cooperation between the fund and other development financing agencies (such as the Kuwait Fund, the Arab Fund and the World Bank group). The recent trend toward more professionalization in the fund's work furthers the prospects for cooperation among the three Arab funds because it emphasizes the technical aspects on which wider agreement can be reached. At the same time, the perceived need for cooperation among the three Arab funds by the policy makers in Abu Dhabi reinforces the tendency toward more professionalization in the Abu Dhabi Fund.

The Project and Policy Process

The preceding discussion of politics in the fund's operations provides the background for analyzing the project and policy process in the Abu Dhabi

Fund. It is obvious that the fund is starting to assign greater significance to the professionalization of its work. This means giving more attention to the process of identifying, selecting, and appraising development projects in the borrowing countries. The experience of the Abu Dhabi Fund in project selection is dominated by an ad hoc approach to the project financing cycle. The fund does not play an active role in terms of project identification in borrower countries. Considering the limited technical resources available in the fund, an active role in project identification represents an enormous demand on the fund's manpower resources that cannot be satisfactorily met in the coming few years. The fund realizes that this shortcoming can be met now and in the immediate future through more collaboration with other development financing institutions, especially the World Bank group. It is commonly recognized in the Abu Dhabi Fund (and also in both the Kuwait and Arab Funds) that the projects for which loan applications are made may not be the best projects available for financing. The reasons a country submits a loan application to one of the funds are numerous. Not all loan applications represent actual developmental needs based on an analysis of the economy that identifies bottlenecks or problem areas. The World Bank realized some time ago that all developing countries, in varying degrees, need assistance in identifying, preparing, and appraising the development projects for which external finance is needed. Although this has become a known lesson in international development financing, not all development financing agencies are capable of getting involved in the project cycle from the identification point through selection, preparation, and appraisal of a project. For such a small organization as the Abu Dhabi Fund, this is all the more difficult. However, the need for the three Arab development funds to play an active role in the project cycle presents an opportunity where cooperation among the three funds can be highly rewarding for them and for the region as well. An active role in identifying, preparing, and appraising high-priority projects could be achieved through the pooling of expertise among the three funds. This aspect will be discussed later in the study.

Table 2.2 above shows the general characteristics of the Abu Dhabi Fund loans, which carry an interest rate of 3-5%. Loans for agricultural development (such as the loan to the Southern Uplands rural development project in the Yemen Arab Republic) and infrastructure (such as loans to King Talal Dam and Al-Azraq road in Jordan) carry a 3% interest charge. Loans to industry (a tin factory project in Tunisia) and tourism (North Sousa tourism project in Tunisia) carry a 5% interest charge. The fund is required by its regulations to collect another 1/2% on its loans in addition to the interest charges to cover its administrative expenses. The grace period in the fund's loans usually ranges from 3.5 years (King Talal Dam project) to 8 years (Southern Uplands rural development project), but for the Sitra power and water station project in Bahrain the grace period is only 1.5 years. The maturity period for the loans ranges from 8 to 22.5 years, depending on the sector of the economy to which the project loan is given and the general economic conditions of the borrowing country. On the basis of interest charges, grace periods, and maturity periods, the grant element included in Abu Dhabi Fund loans ranges between 24% for the tin can factory project in Tunisia and 50% for the Southern Uplands rural development project in the Yemen Arab Republic.(10)

The Abu Dhabi Fund has not been active in extending technical assistance grants for preinvestment studies. Two instances of such grants were as follows:

1. a grant of DH 300,000 to the Yemen Arab Republic for financing a study of the overall development of the Saada and Seham valleys, a study undertaken under the auspices of the Arab Organization for Agricultural Development;

2. a grant of DH 340,000 for an industrial survey to identify potentialities for the development of small- and medium-scale industries in Bahrain. There are indications that the survey reuslted in identifying projects eligible for financing. In January 1976 the fund was proceeding with a DH 100 million loan for small industries to Bahrain.

It is the policy of the Abu Dhabi Fund to extend loans and equity participation only to government-owned (public) projects, unless the governments guarantee repayment of loans to projects within their countries.

Development Strategy

The question of a development strategy is important for the purposes of this study. In the context of regional cooperation and integration, the existence of an identifiable strategy designed to achieve certain objectives is necessary. A strategy usually entails translating certain policy goals into operational steps that may logically fulfill such policy goals. To identify a development strategy in the Abu Dhabi Fund it is revealing to look at the distribution of its loans and equity participations to different sectors of the economy, as shown in Table 2.3.

According to Table 2.3, electricity and water supply projects have constituted more than half of the total lending of the Abu Dhabi Fund. The head of the research department explained the concentration of the Fund's lending in infrastructure as follows: "adequate economic infrastructure is an essential prerequisite to the economic development of any nation. Moreover, the construction of such vast and important projects requires a huge volume of capital on concessionary terms."(11) Such an explanation may give the impression that an integrated development strategy exists in the fund's work. The concentration on infrastructure projects, however, did not result from an extensive debate of policy alternatives and does not formulate an identifiable development strategy for the Abu Dhabi Fund. Infrastructure projects are the traditional area for development financing by most international lending agencies. Until a few years ago, the World Bank group emphasized infrastructure as the favored sector for its lending. This view influenced the policies of most regional and international lending agencies, including those in the Arab region. Although the World Bank group, especially the International Development Association (IDA), has shifted its emphasis to such areas as rural development, education, and family planning, these developments have not influenced the policies of Arab lending agencies, including the Abu Dhabi Fund. The present situation in the Abu Dhabi Fund and in the other two Arab

TABLE 2.3. LOANS AND EQUITY PARTICIPATION OF ABU DHABI FUND
BY SECTOR OF THE ECONOMY, AS OF DECEMBER 31, 1975

Sector	No. of Projects	Amounts of Loans (millions DH)	%
Agriculture	1	40.0	9.8
Manufacturing	3	52.0	12.8
Electricity and Water Supply	4	226.0	55.4
Building and Construction	2	26.5	6.5
Tourism	2	49.7	12.2
Transportation	1	13.5	3.3
TOTAL	13	407.7	100.0

Source: Abu Dhabi Fund for Arab Economic Development, First Annual
Report 1974-75, p. 44.

funds mostly reflects individual efforts by the various funds in pursuing
loosely coordinated priorities. A significant debate on development strategy
has not been intensively conducted by the funds. Many answers explain why
such dabate on strategy has not taken place. In the Abu Dhabi Fund, the
preoccupation with day-to-day operations and an increasing volume of work
to be handled by a limited professional staff hardly leave enough time and
manpower resources for such a debate. Moreover, the financial resources of
the Abu Dhabi Fund are relatively small to allow the fund to influence
development performance in the region through adopting a strategy. The
forum from which a development strategy can emerge is possible when the
three Arab funds covered in this study (and possibly the Saudi and Iraqui
development funds) pool their expertise and experiences together. The debate
on a development strategy in a cooperative context among the development
financing agencies in the region would then represent a first step toward an
identifiable development strategy in which the various funds could contribute
on financial, functional, and geographical bases.

3 The Arab Fund
For Economic and
Social Development

On May 16, 1968, the Economic Council of the League of Arab States adopted the text of the Articles of Agreement Establishing the Arab Fund for Economic and Social Development, which was later signed by seventeen Arab countries. The signatories included Algeria, Bahrain, Egypt, Iraq, Jordan, Kuwait, Lebanon, Libya, Morocco, Qatar, Saudi Arabia, Sudan, Syria, Tunisia, the United Arab Emirates, and both North and South Yemen.

The Arab Fund signifies the desire of the Arab member countries to cooperate for their benefit as a group. Their endeavor in this regard is similar to those that culminated in the creation of the African, Asian, and Inter-American development banks.

Although the agreement establishing the Arab Fund was adopted in 1968, the fund did not begin its operational phase until February 1972 when the board of governors held its first meeting in Kuwait. The present membership of the fund includes, in addition to the original seventeen members, the Somali Republic, Mauritania, Oman, and Palestine (represented by the Palestine Liberation Organization).

The initial authorized capital of the fund was 100 million Kuwaiti dinars divided into 10,000 shares, each valued at KD 10,000. The present subscription by members to the authorized capital is shown in Table 3.1.

This present distribution of shares among members is based on a decision by the board of governors during its fourth annual meeting (1975) to increase the authorized capital to 400 million Kuwaiti dinars. It was left to each member to decide how many shares it would subscribe toward the increase in the fund's capital. Each member subscribes to its share of the capital in two equal installments of 10% of the value of the shares, paid on ratification and on the agreement's going into force. The remaining amount was to be paid in ten equal annual installments.(1) However, the board of governors in its third annual meeting in 1974 reduced by half the remaining period for payment of the subscribed capital.

In the following two sections, we discuss the Arab Fund management, and its policies and operations.

40

TABLE 3.1. SUBSCRIPTION TO AUTHORIZED CAPITAL
OF THE ARAB FUND

Member	Shares
Kuwait	7500
Saudi Arabia	7400
Libya	4776
Egypt	4050
Algeria	3000
Iraq	2941
United Arab Emirates	2000
Syria	1200
Jordan	800
Oman	800
Morocco	800
Sudan	588
Qatar	400
Tunisia	200
Yemen Arab Republic	200
Lebanon	200
Bahrain	100
Mauritania	40
Palestine	25
Somalia	20
Peoples' Democratic Republic of Yemen	4
TOTAL	37044

THE MANAGEMENT OF THE ARAB FUND

As a multilateral development organization, the Arab Fund is managed on the principle that each member country should have a degree of control over the fund commensurate with that country's financial contribution to the fund's capital. This principle is reflected in the voting power given the representative of each country in the board of governors. Each member appoints a governor and alternate governor to the board of governors of the fund, and the governor enjoys the voting power that his country represents. The voting power of each member is a combination of 200 votes (an equalizing flat rate for each member) plus one vote for each share the country has in the fund's capital. Thus, the voting power of the members ranges from 204 votes for the People's Democratic Republic of Yemen to 7,700 votes for Kuwait.

The Arab Fund is managed through two layers of decision-making units: the board of governors, which is the highest policy and decision unit, and the board of directors, which executes the policies formed by the board of governors. The president of the Arab Fund is chairman of the board of directors, who provides the link between the two tiers of decision units. He is the head of the employees in the Arab Fund and represents the fund in its dealing with member governments and other national and international bodies.

The Board of Governors

Each member appoints a governor and an alternate governor for a five-year period, renewable, to represent the state in the board's annual meetings. Each member country, however, can change its governor or alternate at any time.

The board of governors holds annual meetings and elects a chairman annually. The board can be convened upon the request of at least three members who muster 25% of the total number of votes, or upon the request of the board of directors. A quorum for holding any meeting is attained when a majority of the members representing two-thirds of the total number of votes is present.

The board of governors is the highest policy organ for the fund. However, in many instances, the board of directors and the fund's administration initiate policies which are later legitimized or rejected in the annual governors meeting. As a multilateral organization, the Arab Fund can undertake certain functions only by the board of governors, while delegating the rest to the board of directors. Board of governors functions include accepting new members, authorizing increases in the capital, suspending a member state, resolving disputes related to interpretation of the articles of agreement, concluding treaties with other international institutions aimed at increasing cooperation with such institutions, and dissolving the Arab Fund – terminating its operations and specifying how the Arab Fund's net income be dispensed with.

At the first meeting of the board of governors in Kuwait City in February 1972, the board elected the governor representing Kuwait to be its chairman for the following year. At each annual meeting, a new chairman is elected for a one-year period.

The Board of Directors

The board of directors conducts the management of the fund's activities within the guidelines set by the board of governors. Elected by the board of governors for a renewable term of two years, the board of directors consists of six full-time "Arab citizens of recognized experience and competence."(2) For each of the six directors, an alternate is elected by the board of governors. After each governor nominates a person for director and another for alternate, the six directors and their alternates are elected in a majority vote by the board of governors.

The voting power of each governor, as indicated earlier, depends on the financial contribution his country makes to the total capital of the Arab Fund. A quorum for a meeting of the board of directors is attained when directors representing two-thirds of the total number of votes are present. Decisions of the board of directors are reached in a majority vote.

The President

The board of governors appoints the president of the Arab Fund. The president is not chosen from among the governors, alternate governors, directors, or alternate directors of the Arab Fund.

The president chairs the board of directors and heads the employees of the Arab Fund. He does not vote on board of director decisions except when the votes are equally divided.(3) The president attends meetings of the board of governors and takes part in their deliberations but has no voting rights in those meetings.

It has been noted that in multinational organizations similar to the Arab Fund (e.g., the World Bank, the Asian Development Bank, and the Inter-American Development Bank), "the president emerges as the key figure."(4) The president in such an organizational arrangement could have a remarkable influence on the way an institution is staffed and operated. This is true, for example, in the World Bank.(5)

The president of the Arab Fund, Saeb Jaroudi, combines high-level experience in development lending (former deputy director general in the Kuwait Fund) and in policy-making (previously minister of economy and tourism in the Lebanese government). Because of such a background and long-established relationships, the president of the Arab Fund is able to draw upon the cooperation of prominent Arab development experts and also to secure the cooperation of Arab finance and development institutions in the region, particularly those related to the Arab League system.

The president of the Arab Fund, as the head of its employees, has the ultimate administrative authority in the fund within the framework of the personnel regulations approved by the board of directors.

Internal Organization

The main responsibility for the internal organization of the Arab Fund lies with its president, as the main figure representing fund administration. However, the president works within broad personnel policies approved by the board of directors.

As in all multilateral organizations, representation from member countries is necessary on the fund staff.(6) This affects the fund's recruitment policies and limits the freedom of the Arab Fund's management in a way not faced by the Abu Dhabi or Kuwait Funds.

The Arab Fund is still debating various internal organizational structures to choose the most appropriate for its special needs. Figure 3.1 shows the thinking in the fund as of September 1977 concerning its structure.

The Arab Fund has two main operational departments: the programs and the projects departments. Earlier in its operations, the Arab Fund utilized the expertise of senior Arab professionals seconded from international organizations (e.g., the World Bank, the United Nations, etc.). These experts were later integrated in the organization of the fund.

The main professional tasks of the fund are divided between the programs and projects departments. The programs department provides the policy staff duties for the development lending agency and subsumes the research functions undertaken by research departments in similar organizations. The projects department is involved in project evaluation and in the various phases of project implementation and supervision. It also contributes toward fomulating overall lending policies of the fund.

In order to further clarify the evolving distinction between the two departments, it should be emphasized that the main thrust in the work of the programs department concerns identifying long-term development issues in the Arab region. In policy terms, its functions revolve around the formulation of policies, strategies, and programs that deal with these issues. After such a general task is performed, the more immediate task of the programs department is to explore various alternatives and to design the means through which the Arab Fund could promote Arab regional development.

The main concern of the projects department, on the other hand, is to focus on the operational aspects of the fund's work, especially the formulation of lending programs, the identification, preparation, appraisal, and supervision of country projects. A new unit that deals with the operational aspects of intercountry programs has been created. According to information supplied by the Arab Fund in September 1977, the new unit is under the supervision of the vice-president for operations, who also supervises the work of the projects department.

The mandate of the Arab Fund and the ambitious tasks in the area of Arab regional development that the fund aspires to achieve require a vast reservoir of both technical and financial resources. One constraint is the limited pool of highly qualified professionals in the Arab World. The Arab Fund competes with other national and regional organizations for the services of the available Arab professionals in this limited pool. Table 3.2 shows the makeup of this staff.

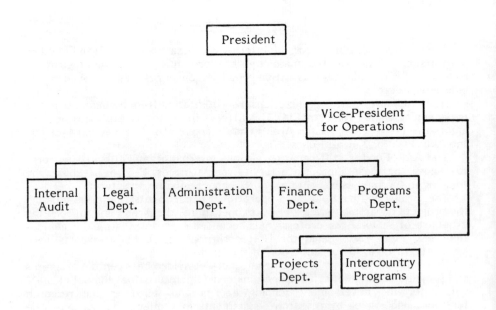

FIG. 3.1. ORGANIZATION CHART OF THE ARAB FUND
(Proposed, September 1977)

TABLE 3.2. STAFF COMPOSITION OF THE ARAB FUND*

| | Actual Staff | | Budgeted Staff | |
	Profes-sionals	General Services	Profes-sionals	General Services
Office of the President	1	2	1	2
Programs Department	9	10	11	8
Projects Department	10	4	11	8
Finance Department	3	15	3	13
Legal Department	4	2	4	3
Administration Department	3	11	3	13
Internal Audit	0	0	1	2
Total (end 1975)	30	44	34	49
Total (end 1976)	40	62	45	62
Total (Sept. 1977)	59	69	57	78

*Information supplied by the Arab Fund.

In a situation where financial resources are not easily increased (since the increase has to come from a multitude of governments, some of which are in perennial deficit, and since market borrowing by the fund would compromise its most needed concessionary loans), and because the possibility to increase the technical staff is rather limited, it seems that the Arab Fund would be better able to fulfill its objectives as a regional development organization by concentrating on a core of activities that would most effectively use its financial and technical resources.

Here we suggest two lines of development for the Arab Fund in which a precise core of activities is defined. We recognize that these suggestions may entail an expansive definition of the articles of agreement, but we are certain that the suggestions fall in line with the spirit which prompted the creation of the Arab Fund. In the face of the financial and technical restraints upon the Arab Fund, it is possible to consider these two lines of development:

1. To distinguish itself among other development lending institutions, the Arab Fund may concentrate only on regional and integrative functions. Recruitment and personnel policies in this perspective could be modeled to build the fund's capabilities in the area of regional and integrative projects and programs. In this way, the difficulties in recruitment and internal organization could be mitigated because the scope of activities would be more limited and more precisely defined.

The wide scope of activities for the fund, which include both extensive country project lending and the development of new initiatives in regional programs and projects, would then be coherently focused on a core of regional and integrative functions.

2. The fund could play an increasing role as coordinator for development lending activities in the region, while de-emphasizing actual involvement in project and program financing. This would enable the fund to utilize its limited staff resources for policy and coordination work. As a cofinancier, the fund can utilize its financial resources to influence what the development lending institutions are doing in the region. The Arab Fund's financial resources (which are relatively limited) could have an enhanced impact on the region by cofinancing projects and programs that already fit in a development policy scheme prepared by the Arab Fund and accepted by other financial institutions in the area.

Both alternatives have drawbacks and require certain preconditions in order to be operational. By concentrating on the regional and integrative programs and projects and de-emphasizing the conventional country-projects approach to development lending, the Arab Fund would be required to initiate, innovate, and abandon the secure shelters of conventional wisdom in development financing. Although such an innovative approach would not require a large number of professionals, it emphasizes the quality and caliber of those recruited.   In addition, the perceived integrative projects and programs would have to gain political support among member states of the fund. Such political support would have to come from both major capital-rich donor states and capital-poor recipient countries.

The other alternative that emphasizes the fund's policy function and coordination role requires certain preconditions too. Although the professional staff could be limited if the fund concentrated on policy and coordination functions, such staff would have to project high standards of competence and tact so that the rest of development financing institutions would accept the policy role and coordination function that the Arab Fund undertakes. The Arab Fund must also persuade development lending agencies in the region to accept the rationale behind its institutional role as a policy-initiating agency. The role of the fund as a coordinator of development-lending activities implies certain mandates that the national aid agencies (e.g., the Kuwait, Iraq, Saudi Arabia, and the Abu Dhabi funds) would have to relinquish to the Arab Fund.

Both alternatives have risks that could be encountered in implementing them. Nonetheless, the Arab Fund would be jeopardizing the efficient use of its resources if it "spreads itself too thin"; the Fund has to find a focus for its activities.

POLICIES AND OPERATIONS

Compared with the Kuwait and Abu Dhabi Funds, the Arab Fund is a more recent organization. Although the Arab Fund was established as a functioning organization in 1972, it was not until February 1974 that its first three loan agreements were signed. During 1975, 18 more loan agreements were signed, and by the end of 1976 the total volume of lending amounted to KD. 170.2 million distributed among 31 loans in various Arab countries, as shown in Table 3.3.

As indicated earlier, the Arab Fund looks ahead toward assuming an ambitious role in the context of development lending in the region. The available resources of the fund, especially in manpower, would make it imperative for the fund to concentrate on a certain area of activity.

In an important policy statement, the first chairman of the board of governors identified three main tasks for the fund: 1) to find and promote mutually beneficial opportunities for cooperation among its members, basically in identifying joint Arab projects that would promote Arab economic integration; 2) to attract Arab professionals living abroad to come and work in the area for the sake of Arab development; 3) to seek opportunities in the Arab region for the investment of surplus Arab funds.(7)

In the past years, the Arab Fund has undertaken innovative and bold initiatives to fulfill some of the tasks enumerated above. However, the bulk of the fund's financing remains in the conventional area of country projects, an area where national aid agencies are able to do more by virtue of their larger financial resources and political preferences.

In the next three sections we deal with politics in the Arab Fund, its project and policy process, and its development strategy.

Politics of the Arab Fund

The political setup in the Arab Fund differs from that found in national aid agencies such as the Kuwait and Abu Dhabi Funds. There is no monolith political interest to be served. Rather, politics in the Arab Fund activities is manifested in the need to balance the interest of the various members. This process of balancing various interests requires attention to the attitudes of major capital contributors (such as Kuwait and Saudi Arabia) and of major recipients, whose attitudes are politically significant for the viability of the fund (such as Egypt and the Sudan). The delicate process of balancing various considerations demands political awareness and diplomatic skills from the fund's administration. However, there is a rationale behind the creation of the Arab Fund: the existence of a community of interests among the Arab countries. Although the fund is created to promote common economic interests, it is acknowledged that a common political will is required for the Arab Fund to operate effectively. By entering into the area of integration projects and programs, the Arab Fund offers its members the opportunity to test the strength of their common political will.

As in most multilateral agencies, the Arab Fund is prohibited from using any kind of political criteria in dispensing its funds. The president and staff of the fund "must not allow themselves to be influenced by any consideration other than the interest of the fund, and they shall remain impartial in the discharge of their duties."(8) This impartiality is required in an environment where sometimes incompatible political attitudes exist. A central problem of multilateral agencies is that "they lack effective political power"(9) to back up their programs. This lack of political power represents one side of a coin,

TABLE 3.3. PROJECT LOANS OF
THE ARAB FUND FOR ECONOMIC AND SOCIAL DEVELOPMENT

	Year of Loan Agreement	Loan Amount KD (m.)	Lending Conditions %	Grace Period	Maturity
ALGERIA					
New Arzew port	1974	.66	6.0	5	25
telecommunications (Algeria-Morocco joint project)	1975	.33	6.0	4	22
EGYPT					
Tourah cement expansion	1975	6.7	6.0	5	25
Talka II fertilizers	1974	6.5	6.0	5	25
Cairo/Fostat water supply	1975	9.7	6.0	5	20
Sewerage for Helwan City	1975	8.3	6.0	6	20
Talka II fertilizers (supplementary)	1976	2.7	4.0	3	17
Abu Qir power station expansion	1976	12.0	4.0	5	20
Kafr El Dawar textile	1976	10.0	4.0	5	20
JORDAN					
Amman road construction	1975	5.0	6.0	4	20
Electric power development	1976	6.0	6.0	5	20
MOROCCO					
Telecommunications (Algeria-Morocco joint project)	1975	3.0	6.0	4	20
Beni Amir irrigation	1976	7.0	6.0	5	20
SUDAN					
Gadaref-Kassala highway	1974	8.0	4.0	6	25
telecommunication	1975	4.8	4.0	4	24
Rahad Road	1975	4.4	4.0	5	20
Sennar-Damazin highway	1976	11.0	4.0	6	20
SYRIA					
Underground fuel reservoirs	1974	2.0	5.0	5	25
Livestock development (cattle)	1975	5.4	6.0	4	20
Damascus water supply	1976	12.0	6.0	5	15
TUNISIA					
Tunis-Sud electric power	1974	2.0	6.0	4	20
El Barma gas	1975	4.0	6.0	3	20

(Table 3.3 Continued)

	Year of Loan Agreement	Loan Amount KD (m.)	Lending Conditions		
			%	Grace Period	Maturity
YEMEN (Arab Rep.)					
Electric power	1974	4.0	4.0	5	20
Water supply and sewerage	1975	6.0	4.0	5	20
Aden-Taiz highway	1976	3.8	4.0	5	25
YEMEN (Democratic Rep.)					
Mukalla multipurpose	1974	3.2	4.0	5	20
Mukalla (supplementary)	1976	2.6	4.0	3	17
Aden port rehabilitation	1975	3.9	4.0	3	20
Aden-Taiz highway	1976	6.5	4.0	5	25
MAURITANIA					
Power station	1976	5.2	4.0	5	25
Highway project	1976	7.0	4.0	5	25
SOMALIA					
Inter-riverine settlement	1976	6.4	4.0	5	25
OMAN					
Gas utilization	1976	6.0	6.0	3	16

Source: The Arab Fund for Economic and Social Development.

the other side of which is impartiality. Multilateral agencies can only persuade and exhort members to accept their programs and to go along with ideas that such members would later bear the price for. We mentioned earlier the need for the Arab Fund to be innovative and to be able to engender bold initiatives that work for economic integration among its member countries. The Arab Fund can be successful in those areas only insofar as it can persuade its various members, represented by their top financial officials in the board of governors, of the value of such programs. Since multilateral agencies lack political authority they would have to substitute other forms of authority. In the Arab region, a 'moral' authority is called for. The divergent political interests of various countries in the Arab region would have to be transcended occasionally for regional and integration efforts to succeed.

The Project and Policy Process

Most of the loans concluded by the Arab Fund since it started operations were given to country projects as shown in Table 3.3. In the Arab region there will always be a need for country project financing because many of the Arab countries have perennial shortages in hard currencies to finance imports for their development projects.

Country projects are also easy to appriase by use of conventional cost-benefit techniques such as discount cash flows and internal rates of return. In many instances in the Arab region, such country projects would have already secured an external financier (such as the World Bank) to provide technical assistance. In such cases the financing institution in the region (whether it is the Arab, the Kuwait, or the Abu Dhabi Fund) is concerned mainly with the financing aspects of the loan.

Nonetheless, the Arab Fund in two instances played an important role as a catalyst for the mobilization of Arab and international funds. In the case of Talkha II project (Egypt) and the New Arzew port (Algeria), the Arab Fund was able to attract financial resources from other institutions in the region and abroad that amounted to three times its own contributions.(10)

The Arab Fund's role in financing the Talkha II project is particularly significant as an example of an active role in cofinancing, which was mentioned earlier.(11)

Financing the foreign currency cost of the Talkha II project was undertaken through joint financing among Arab lenders and parallel financing with the International Development Association (IDA).(12) The amounts of the loans (in millions) that each cofinancier contributed were as follows:

Arab Fund: KD 6.5 with 6% interest;
Kuwait Fund: KD 7.0 with 4% interest;
Abu Dhabi Fund: KD 3.0 with 4.5% interest;
Libyan Arab Foreign Bank: KD 3.0 with 6.5% interest;
Government of Qatar: KD 1.0 with 6.5% interest;
IDA (World Bank): KD 6.0 with 0.75% service charge.

The joint financing of the Arab lenders took two forms. For the three development funds (Kuwait, Abu Dhabi, and Arab Funds), a regular lending arrangement was undertaken, and money was disbursed to the recipient's credit as expenses were incurred. For the Libyan Bank and Government of Qatar loans, the Arab Fund sold bonds on behalf of the recipient country to both lenders in the amounts of their loans. The amounts were credited to the borrower for use in connection with the project. The bonds were sold to both lenders (Libyan Bank and Qatar) in their local currencies. The Arab Fund would then receive the proceeds of the bonds as a party who is absorbing the foreign exchange fluctuation risk, relieving the borrower (Egypt) from such a risk.

As Table 3.3 shows, the interest rates the Arab Fund charges on its loans range between 4 and 6%. The Arab Fund tries to keep uniform the interest charges for two types of projects: 6% for standard loans, and 4% special concessionary loans. The interest rate depends on the state of the economy of the borrowing country and the sector in which the project falls. Most of the concessionary loans were given to infrastructure projects.

All of the Arab Fund loans were country project loans, except for the loan to Morocco and Algeria of KD 6.3 million for expanding the telephone network connecting the two countries. Table 3.4 shows the distribution of Arab Fund loans by country and sector, and Table 3.5 shows distribution by sector and country's level of development.

TABLE 3.4. DISTRIBUTION OF ARAB FUND'S LENDING OPERATIONS
BY BENEFICIARY ARAB COUNTRY AND SECTOR OF THE ECONOMY
AS OF DECEMBER 12, 1976
(KD. million)

	Transport and Communications	Water and Sewerage	Electricity	Manufacturing Industries	Agriculture and Settlements	Gas, Storage, and Oil	Telecommunications	Total
Hashemite Kingdom of Jordan	5.0	–	6.0	–	–	–	–	11.0
Republic of Tunisia	–	–	2.0	–	–	4.0	–	6.0
Algerian Dem. and People's Rep.	6.0	–	–	–	–	–	0.3	6.3
Dem. Republic of Sudan	23.4	–	–	–	–	–	4.8	28.2
Syrian Arab Republic	–	12.0	–	–	5.4	2.0	–	19.4
Arab Republic of Egypt	–	18.0	12.0	25.9	–	–	–	55.9
Yemen Arab Republic	3.8	6.0	4.0	–	–	–	–	13.8
Kingdom of Morocco	–	–	–	–	7.0	–	3.0	10.0
People's Dem. Rep. of Yemen	13.5	–	1.0	1.7	–	–	–	16.2
Somali Democratic Republic	–	–	–	–	6.4	–	–	6.4
Islamic Republic of Mauritania	7.0	–	5.2	–	–	–	–	12.2
Sultanate of Oman	–	–	–	–	–	6.0	–	6.0
TOTAL	58.7	36.0	30.2	27.6	18.8	12.0	8.1	191.4
% of sector to total loans	30.7	18.8	15.8	14.4	9.8	6.3	4.2	100.0

Source: The Arab Fund for Economic and Social Development

TABLE 3.5. DISTRIBUTION OF ARAB FUND LOANS
BY SECTOR AND LEVEL OF DEVELOPMENT DURING 1976

	Least Developed Arab Countries (KD million)	Other Arab Countries (KD million)	Total (KD million)	%
Transport and communications	28.9	–	28.9	29.4
Electricity	5.7	18.0	23.7	24.1
Water and Sewerage	–	12.0	12.0	12.2
Total	34.6	30.0	64.6	65.7
Manufacturing industries	1.5	12.7	14.2	14.5
Agriculture and settlements	6.4	7.0	13.4	13.7
Gas	–	6.0	6.0	6.1
Total	7.9	25.7	33.6	34.3
Grand Total	42.5	55.7	98.2	100
%	43.3	56.7	–	100

Source: The Arab Fund for Economic and Social Development

Although the articles of agreement of the Arab Fund does not limit the amount of a loan in relation to total project costs or on the type of project-cost to be financed by such a loan (i.e., foreign currency component vs. local expenditure component), the fund has concentrated on financing the import components of its projects.(13)

The Arab Fund, like other financing institutions in the region, recognizes that the process of project identification and preparation can be vastly improved.(14) To give proper attention to this aspect, the board of governors decided in its second annual meeting, 1973, to create an Investment Servicing and Promotion Unit (ISPU). Accordingly, the fund established the unit in 1974, within its programs department. This unit is expected to:

a) prepare an inventory of investment opportunities and project profiles;

b) assist in working out model forms of participation agreements and related basic systems, and in attracting such technical and managerial know-how as may be required for the implementation of such projects;

c) stimulate the flow of project oriented funds to member countries from within the area and outside, with emphasis on encouraging the flow of funds from Arab countries with a large potential of investment oriented capital.(15)

Although ISPU is expected to concentrate on the latter function, its work can improve the identification and preparation phases of the project. Since private capital is sought in most of the investment opportunities to be identified by ISPU, the Arab Fund would still face problems of identification and preparation of development projects in spheres where private capital is reluctant to enter (e.g., integration or multicountry projects). There is some consideration in the fund for establishing a new department (lending operations department) to handle the tasks associated with the identification and preparation of development projects in member countries.

Development Strategy

A major reason behind establishing the Arab Fund was the need for a financing institution that approaches development projects with an emphasis on the regional and integrative inter-Arab aspects. The agreement establishing the fund stipulates that preference should be given in the fund's work to economic projects that are vital to the Arab entity and to joint Arab projects.(16)

The Arab Fund has started some initiatives in that direction. Three years ago, and with the cooperation of the United Nations Development Program (UNDP), the fund started financing a preinvestment study to develop a master plan for a Pan-Arab telecommunications network. As a result, the fund provided a loan to Morocco and Algeria to establish an automatic telephone network between the two countries. The Arab Fund is also preparing a preliminary study to develop a master plan for a Pan-Arab surface transportation system, in order to identify portions that would be eligible for project loans.(17)

After discussions and negotiations, in December 1975 the Arab Fund and UNDP signed a six-year agreement for setting up an integrated program for the identification and evaluation of inter-Arab projects. The agreement would allow UNDP and the Arab Fund to finance preinvestment and feasibility studies for such projects. The Arab Fund would be the executing agency for UNDP, according to this program, which allows for close cooperation between UNCTAD, the fund, and the Council for Arab Economic Unity.(18) The objective of this undertaking is to identify priority for regional projects that are significant for achieving Arab economic integration.

Another major initiative of the Arab Fund is for agriculture development in the Sudan, developed in consultations between the fund and the Sudanese government. The fund's interest in the program comes from the expected regional benefits that would result when the program is implemented. The Sudan program aims at increasing the production of certain agricultural commodities such as grain, cotton, and sugar. According to these objectives, the Sudan will be able to produce agricultural commodities and food items not only for its own requirements, but to meet the regional needs for such products. On this understanding, the board of directors of the fund approved in April 1974 a technical assistance budget for financing the preparation of the program, which was undertaken by an interdisciplinary task force.

In recognition of the shortage of capital as a crucial impediment to agricultural development in the Sudan,(19) the program represents an ambitious effort for the implementation of one hundred projects over a ten-year span. The preliminary estimates for the total cost of the program is 2,287 million Sudanese pound (SP),* of which SP 801 million is in local currency and SP 1,486 million is in foreign exchange. The funds needed for the implementation of the program are envisaged to be SP 540 million in equity participation, SP 36 m. in grants, SP 1,143 m. in concessionary loans (4% interest or less), and SP 568 m. in commercial loans and credits. To undertake this program the fund estimates that 32% of the projects would be infrastructure projects and 68% would be in directly productive sectors. This ambitious program is divided into stages (or plans) of which the first plan calls for the investment of KD 780 m.

To undertake the program, an Arab Authority for Agricultural Investment and Development (AAAID) was created in an agreement signed in November 1976 between twelve Arab governments. The capital of the authority, set at KD 150 million, had been 75% subscribed to by the end of 1976.

The first investment plan calls for spending KD 780 million to be distributed as follows: KD 75 million to be contributed by the Sudanese Government for agriculture projects; KD 295 million in infrastructure projects of which KD 44 million comes from commercial loans, KD 240 million in the form of concessionary loans and KD 11 million in grants; KD 410 million in joint ventures to be financed collaboratively among the Authority (40%), the Sudanese Government (40%) and commercial lenders (20%).

To shape this investment plan, the Arab Fund is contacting possible financiers from governments and private commercial institutions. However, the administrative structure and the management posts in AAAID were not settled as of April 1978, which may induce delay in implementing the plan.(20)

Indeed, the image of the Arab Fund as a multilateral institution raises the hopes that its work would concentrate more on the type of regional and integrative efforts exemplified in the Sudan program and the joint inter-country investment undertaking. In terms of financing, the Arab Fund is still heavily involved in country projects, as Table 3.3 clearly indicates. Most of these country projects are infrastructural, which allows them, indirectly, to facilitate the development and integration of the region.

In view of the increasing interest by the fund in new modalities for programs that aim at further interlinking of the various Arab economies, however, it is hoped that future financing activities by the fund would support more types of integrative programs similar to the one in the Sudan. Notwithstanding the value of infrastructure country projects and their indirect contribution to regional development, we believe that it is the truly integrative programs that would give the Arab Fund its distinctive character-istic among development financing institutions in the region.

---

*According to official rates of exchange (April 1978), SP = $2.91.

4 The Arab Funds and Regional Development

The Arab region, among other developing regions, is particularly endowed with common cultural and historical denominators. The factors that bind the Arab countries together are numerous, paramount among them being language, culture, common history, and joint aspirations.(1) The attempts to articulate the Arab regional identity in recent times emerged on the political level, with the creation of the League of Arab States in 1945. The Arab League, which started as a collective security organization, developed in time to perform wider functions.

Although political cooperation among the Arab countries is given the highest priority in view of the Arab-Israeli conflict, other forms of cooperation are gaining increasing significance. The Arab League system, as a cooperation mechanism, has penetrated the economic and social fields as well. The expansion of the League system was evidenced in the creation of the Council for Arab Economic Unity (CAEU) and a host of specialized agencies such as the Arab Labour Organization (ALO), the Industrial Development Centre for the Arab States (IDCAS), and, more recently, the Arab Monetary Fund (AMF).

The increase in oil revenues for some Arab countries after 1973 has given Arab regional development an added impetus. The Arab region, with some countries accumulating financial reserves and others suffering from capital shortages while being rich in human and other resources, presents a promising picture for regional development. In economic terms, the elements necessary for a complementary, industrialized and diversified economic structure within the region are present.(2)

A regional approach to Arab development, as opposed to a country approach, is gaining in significance among Arab development experts. The region has a better chance of effecting economic development than at any recent time. Undoubtedly, the oil factor is a major catalyst for regional development. The prospective gains from regionalism should be enough to motivate policy makers who may be reluctant to pursue development on regional terms. The bargaining powers that both oil-exporting and nonoil-exporting Arab countries could gain from a unified regional strategy far exceeds their present ones. A region as a whole is better equipped to exercise influence vis-a-vis the rest of the world than its members separated.(3)

Some economists, advocates of fundamental changes in the existing international economic relationships, believe that Third World countries could not achieve economic and social progress unless they withdraw from the present unequal economic relationship with the developed countries.(4) Self-reliance, as advocated in this view, would have a better chance of effecting progress if it is undertaken on a regional rather than a national level. In such a setup, "the conditions will be achieved for cultural and intellectual cooperation which in itself can only be considered positive."(5)

Regardless of the ideological views advocated, the gains from regionalism in the Arab world cannot be ignored. Such gains are recognized not only by the professional economists or academicians, but also by the policy makers involved in Arab problems. In a recent report to the Council for Arab Economic Unity, its secretary general indicated that the creation of an Arab economic grouping would facilitate the transfer of technology to the Arab region, increase confidence in the Arab region in international economic and financial circles, and generally increase the Arab bargaining power.(6)

In this chapter, we shall discuss the prospects for Arab regional development. We begin by dealing with the effectiveness of comprehensive integration schemes as a framework for Arab regional cooperation and development. We shall demonstrate that the shortcomings of such comprehensive schemes of economic integration have led to the emergence of a more limited approach to economic cooperation and regional development. We then discuss what we consider a burgeoning Arab regional strategy in which the contributions of the Arab funds play an important role. Finally, we deal with the role of the United Nations system in promoting Arab regional development.

EFFECTIVENESS OF COMPREHENSIVE INTEGRATION SCHEMES

The movement toward integration in the developing countries through generalized trade liberalization (i.e., comprehensive integration schemes) has not produced any particularly bright or successful examples. Political as well as economic difficulties surround the implementation of comprehensive integration schemes based on trade liberalization. The experience of the Arab region is no exception.(7)

The most ambitious attempt at comprehensive integration in the Arab region is exemplified in the Arab Common Market. This was brought about in a resolution of the Council for Arab Economic Unity (CAEU) in August 1964. The Arab Common Market was designed to achieve the following objectives:

1. Freedom of movement of persons and capital.

2. Freedom of exchange of domestic and foreign goods and products.

3. Freedom of residence, work, employment, and exercise of economic activity.

4. Freedom of transport and transit and of use of the means of transportation and of ports and civil airports.(8)

Members of the Arab Common Market included Syria, Iraq, Kuwait, Jordan, Egypt, North Yemen, and the Sudan. The agreement provided for the member countries to liberalize trade in agricultural and industrial products, and provide for the free movement of factors of production (labor and capital in successive stages. The agreement also permitted any member to present a list of goods and services to be exempted temporarily from tariff reduction and/or the removal of quantitative restrictions as designated in the agreement.

Kuwait failed to become a member by not ratifying the agreement, and Yemen was permitted to become merely an observer. Other countries (Jordan, Syria, Iraq, and Egypt) restricted their participation in the agreement by asking for a large number of their products to be exempted from the reduction of tariffs and the removal of quantitative restrictions.(9)

Probably one of the thorniest issues in any economic integration scheme based on generalized trade liberalization concerns the distribution of costs and benefits among the partners.(10) Free trade usually enhances the benefits of the most industrialized among the group of developing countries in the integration. It would also hurt member countries who depend on customs duties as a major source of public revenues. It was observed that a likely reason behind the lack of enthusiasm in implementing the Arab common market agreement is the heavy costs such an implementation would represent to some members. Jordan would face a substantial loss in foreign exchange revenues coming from customs duties, and Syria and the Sudan would suffer higher unemployment in their industrial sectors due to their inability to compete effectively with the relatively advanced industrial sector in Egypt.(11) Although such imbalances could be redressed through the designation of a compensatory mechanism, such a mechanism is usually cumbersome and difficult to agree upon among integration partners. Besides, there is always an element of uncertainty in integration: "The short-term benefits of national protection are present and certain, whereas those of opening new markets in neighbor countries are in the future and uncertain."(12)

In studying inter-Arab trade relations and the attempts at comprehensive integration schemes, an observer noted that: a) such integration could prove to be a very effective instrument for regional economic development if it were to involve the wide-ranging resources available in the region; b) such a comprehensive undertaking would require a wide community of political and economic interests and aspirations; c) such a wide community of interests and aspirations has been lacking among the Arab countries.(13)

At face value, it seems that the first two points of his observations are acceptable. However, we disagree with the last one. We believe that there is a community of interests and aspirations among the Arab countries, as evidenced by some recent events.

At least on the political level, the common actions taken by the Arab countries during and immediately after the October 1973 War demonstrate that such a community exists. The Arab governments come to joint actions when they perceive that a certain danger threatens their community of political and eonomic interests. In the case of economic integration, however, the goals of common actions have not been perceived yet as of vital importance to the Arab community of interests. As such, the consequences of not effecting Arab economic integration are not regarded as a real threat facing the Arabs.

Moreover, we think that generalized trade liberalization (as exemplified in the Arab Common Market) is not the appropriate strategy for Arab regional development. There are too many uncertainties about the benefits of such a scheme to make it workable in the Arab region. For example, the more ambitious elements of the Arab Common Market, such as the free movement of labor and capital, require an agreement on a wide spectrum of political and economic matters. Such an agreement may be difficult to achieve instantaneously.

A different strategy for Arab regional development is needed and we suggest that such a strategy is evolving. We think the disappointment with the Arab Common Market would lead to sidestepping comprehensive integration schemes (including trade liberalization), as a strategy for Arab regional development.

A NEW REGIONAL STRATEGY

When economic integration is viewed in the context of the developing countries' endeavors to enhance their economic, social, and cultural well-being, it becomes obvious that the creation of a customs union or a common market is just one option among many. Some economists suggest that economic integration passes through three different stages: cooperation, coordination, and full integration.(14) Economic integration is viewed as an attempt at creating a desirable institutional framework for the optimization of economic policy. Considering the difficulties involved in the comprehensive integration schemes, developing countries may be better off in attempting more limited approaches to integration. Such approaches would be designed to meet the needs of the particular political and economic systems involved and would concentrate on areas where immediate gains could be realized.(15)

The project approach to economic integration has been perceived as an appropriate vehicle for institutional cooperation, and possibly higher integration at a later stage.(16) One apparent advantage for project cooperation is that partners to the schemes of cooperation retain, almost intact, their national control over economic affairs. Second, the gains and losses to the various partners are more readily identified, and agreement on compensatory schemes can be easily reached. Moreover, project cooperation entails embarking on new activities of production and investment in cooperating countries, rather than redistribution and reallocation of existing utilized capacities. This last reason is of particular significance in the Arab region, where efforts to reallocate or redistribute utilized capacities usually entail difficulties, while the increase in the financial resources in the region encourages new ventures.(17)

There are two forms under which project cooperation could form an institutional backdrop for economic integration. The first is called a partial customs union cum investment plan.(18) In such an agreement, the integration partners agree to allocate among themselves a number of industries (covering, for instance, a certain sector), whose products will have free access to the markets of these countries. Such a form of cooperation would be in the interest of countries with a burgeoning, but economically important, industrial sector that may be jeopardized if the countries enter into a comprehensive integration scheme. This arrangement allows developing countries to benefit from selective industrial specialization on a regional level, as well as from the economies of scale brought about by the larger regional markets.

The other form of project cooperation, called integration projects, allows more than one country to combine their factors of production in implementing the project and to share the benefits accruing from it. This form of project cooperation, which is more common than the first one, may have many variations. In an UNCTAD study the following examples of integration (multinational) projects were enumerated:

1. Projects physically located in or between two or more countries that represent a joint investment (e.g., an international bridge, a gas pipeline) or projects which have their headquarters in one country but provide services for two or more countries and are the result of joint investment (e.g., a technical institute).

2. Projects composed of coordinated national subprojects (e.g., a road network or a telecommunications system).

3. Projects located in a single country that entail the use of inputs from and the provision of goods and services to two or more countries (e.g., a basic industry, a port or a canal).

4. Projects located in a single country and of primary interest to that country but which are necessary for maintaining a compensatory balance in the benefits derived from an integration scheme in which such a country is a part.(19)

The Arab region seems to be giving increasing attention to project cooperation in its various forms. Some on-going activities of the Arab Fund, such as the telecommunications project for the Arab region and the basic program for agricultural development in the Sudan, are examples of integration projects as described in the UNCTAD study.

As explained earlier, serious efforts in the Arab region to identify forms of project cooperation are practical, feasible, and beneficial. It has been observed that "collective organisation to serve a limited and specific common purpose seems to have greater practical potential as a way of realising the strength of numbers than more comprehensive and therefore more contentious schemes of economic integration."(20) The Arab Fund as a collective organization has proved to be a source for initiatives in the area of project cooperation. National funds such as the Kuwait, Abu Dhabi, or Saudi funds have not given paramount attention to integration projects in the Arab region; as sources of financing, however, their contributions could be greater than that of the Arab Fund.

The concentration on project and to a lesser extent on program cooperation in the Arab region is, at best, a springboard for a regional strategy. It cannot substitute for a more coordinated effort, on a higher policymaking level, for the discussion, articulation, and implementation of a regional development strategy. The present and the future attempts at project cooperation in which the various Arab funds play a prominent role provide the base on which to build a regional strategy.

The benefits accruing to both donors and recipients of capital assistance in the projects and programs financed by the various Arab funds are important for the development of a more coherent future regional strategy. Looking at such benefits as achievements in the area of economic cooperation, the participants see tangible results of experiences that can be multiplied and built upon.(21)

In addition to project cooperation manifested in the work of the various Arab funds, there are also many commercial joint ventures that combine the resources of various Arab participants. Examples are the Mineral Resource Development Co., with a capital of KD 100 million, and the Livestock Development Co., with a capital of KD 50 million. Also, the Organization of Arab Petroleum Exporting Countries (OAPEC) was instrumental in bringing about four joint economic projects:(22)

1) The Arab Maritime Petroleum Transport Company (AMPTC) was founded on January 6, 1973, with headquarters in Kuwait. The company's authorized capital was fixed at $500 million, raised three years later to $600 million. The subscribed capital is $100 million. The company can undertake all activities of maritime transport of hydrocarbons.

2) The Arab Shipbuilding and Repair Yard (ASRY) came into being on December 1, 1974, headquartered in Bahrain. Its authorized capital has been raised to $300 million with a subscribed capital of $100 million. An estimated 3,000 technical workers are needed to fulfill the first part of the drydock contract.

3) The Arab Petroleum Investment Corporation (AIPC), established on November 23, 1975, with an authorized capital of $1 billion and a subscribed capital of 1.2 million Saudi riyals, is headquartered in Dammam (Saudi Arabia).

4) The Arab Petroleum Services Company (APSC) was founded on January 8, 1977, with headquarters in Tripoli (Libya). Its authorized capital was fixed at 100 million Libyan dinars.

Project cooperation is a major form of inter-Arab economic cooperation at present. It could build the base from which more ambitious regional development schemes may evolve in the future. There are many views, however, concerning the adequacy of the present structure for project cooperation in the Arab region. At the core of this structure, as this study demonstrates, are a number of Arab development funds of national and multilateral character.

On one hand, there are many shortcomings in the present methods of identifying, preparing, appraising, and supervising the projects financed by the Arab funds surveyed in this study. The Abu Dhabi, Kuwait, Saudi, and Arab funds have not institutionalized the procedures by which they identify, appraise, and supervise projects. A main obstacle that impedes the funds from giving the project cycle more serious attention is the shortage of technical staff. Many development lending agencies such as the World Bank, the Asian Development Bank, or the Inter-American Development Bank have given systematic attention and resources to the project cycle in their lending activities.(23) But most of these lending agencies have larger professional staffs, and for some of them (e.g., the World Bank), such systematic attention to the project process took fifteen years to emerge.(24) At any rate, the attention of the Arab funds to the project cycle needs to be increased and institutionalized.

Such a need to improve the preinvestment stage in the Arab funds' lending has led to a proposal for establishing a "Joint Technical Services Center." The proposed center would function as a pool of technical expertise and would entail institutionalizing cooperation among the various Arab funds in technical matters related to project identification, selection, and evaluation. The establishment of the center is the subject of a feasibility study now in progress. If such a center is created, it may result in sharing technical information and efficiently utilizing technical expertise among the various funds. This would be a step in the right direction because it economizes the use of two scarce elements in the Arab region, i.e., qualified professional personnel and reliable socioeconomic data.

Some critics of the present structure for project cooperation believe that it is not conducive to the most efficient utilization of available resources. They indicate that the proliferation of development lending agencies appears to encourage the diffusion of scarce manpower (planners, economists, administrators), prevent the application of uniform criteria for project appraisal both among and within sectors and countries, militate against the formulation of integrated programs of aid to individual recipient countries, increase the cost of aid administration and surveillance, reduce the capability of individual lending agencies to carry out substantive and comprehensive research to foster promising avenues of investment, and increase the donor's nondevelopment considerations, since a national lending institution is more likely to be subject to narrow political pressures.(25) Such views have led some to suggest the integration of the various Arab development funds, national and multilateral, into one Arab development lending institution.(26)

The present shortcomings of the structure for project cooperation, however, would not be overcome by integrating the existing funds into a larger one. Several reasons make such a solution unlikely and, above all, undesirable.

A major consideration behind the creation of the national development funds is political. Abu Dhabi, Kuwait, and Saudi Arabia see a political advantage in maintaining separate funds that are responsive to their own political interests.(27) Such funds perform the important function of enhancing the goodwill and the political prestige of their countries among both Arab and non-Arab developing countries. Such legitimate poltiical interests would be sacrificed if the national funds are integrated into one large Arab fund. In the present political realities of the region, the policy makers in Kuwait, Abu Dhabi, or Riyadh would be recluctant to dissolve their national funds.

These national funds also perform other important nonpolitical functions for their home states. The Kuwait Fund, for example, is considered in some important Kuwaiti circles to perform significantly as "a source of research spin-off and cross-fertilization for Kuwait's investment institutions within the Middle East."(28)

The integration of the national funds into one fund may not only be unlikely, but also undesirable. Creating one large development financing institution in the Arab world may lead to the bureaucratization of the functions of development lending. A large bureaucracy of development lending in the Arab world has many disadvantages. Such a bureaucracy would be difficult to control. It would be susceptible to different and sometimes conflicting national pressures and interests. Moreover, bureaucratization usually promotes inefficiencies that are not checked. Such a development fund may also grow to be unresponsive to regional needs; "an agency which is overwhelmingly the leading source of resources or services in its own particular field is under no great pressure to please the client."(29)

If one large development fund in the Arab world is unlikely and also undesirable for the near future, the question remains concerning the inadequacy of the present structure for project cooperation. Undoubtedly, the existence of several Arab funds competing for a limited pool of qualified Arab professionals and duplicating project missions and other functional activities entails a certain waste of scarce resources. If project cooperation is to establish the strong base on which a more solid and far-reaching regional strategy is to emerge, the present shortcomings have to be remedied.

The realization of the need for coordination among the Arab financing institutions prompted the secretary general of the Arab League to invite the directors of Arab financial institutions to a meeting in Cairo in 1975. There the directors agreed to hold regular meetings among themselves and also to ask the heads of the operational departments in their respective institutions to organize regular meetings among themselves.(30) Such meetings could produce tangible results by reducing the duplication of work or by coordinating functional activities (e.g., project evaluation missions and research activities). Nevertheless, the fact that such meetings are held regularly among the various Arab funds does not mean that coordination follows. Indeed, the outcome of such meetings depends to a great extent on the manner in which the participants perceive these meetings. It also depends on the degree of seriousness and the amount of time spent in preparing for these meetings and in the implementation of decisions taken.

It is too early to evaluate the results of the coordination meetings held within the Arab League system among the development financing institutions. It would be naive, however, to overestimate the effectiveness of these regular coordination meetings in solving problems inherent in the present structure of project cooperation.(31)

One possible way to overcome the waste of resources implicit in the present structure would involve specialization among the various Arab funds along functional or sectoral lines (e.g., agriculture lending, industrial lending, infrastructure, etc.).(32) To implement this suggestion, the various funds would have to accept limiting their activities to certian sectors or types of projects. This may entail some dislocations among the professional staff presently working at the various funds. In addition, since all the three national funds (Kuwait, Abu Dhabi, and Saudi Funds) operate both within and outside the Arab region, some of their operations may involve specialization within the region, while other operations would continue to cover the sectors that these funds have covered before.

We think that complete functional specializations of each of the funds in the Arab region may be difficult in view of the involvement of the national funds in extraregional lending. In order to overcome the present waste of resources, the operations of each of the national funds within the Arab region should be subject, in one form or another, to organizational linkage with other national funds and with the Arab Fund for Economic and Social Development (AFESD).

The organizational linkage among the funds has to be undertaken on two levels, the technical (i.e., information gathering and exchange and research activities concerning certain problems common in the funds' work), and the decision-making level (i.e., decisions on loans, missions, coordination of lending mechanisms, uniform disbursement practices, etc.).

It is evident that the proposal on a "Joint Technical Services Center" can be valuable in handling the organizational link among the various Arab funds on the technical level. The shape of the center and its characteristic functions are matters of discussion at present and have yet to emerge and be accepted by the various funds.

But beyond the technical level, there is also a need to establish or strengthen the organizational links among the various Arab funds on the decision-making and policy levels. Coordination mechanisms in the decision-making area need to be established and institutionalized in order to tackle regular points of contact among the various funds in regard to such functions as professional missions, choice of projects, and negotiation with both Arab and international financial institutions.

Aside from these routine points of contact among the various Arab funds, there is also a need to coordinate strategies on a regional scale. There should be a mechanism for planning future activities that combines resources from the various funds. Such regional planning may deal with policy questions related to program or country lending. The various funds may find it beneficial for them to offer program lending for a certian sector in the Arab region (i.e., food production, heavy industries, road or telecommunications networks). In pooling a certian amount of both financial and technical resources, program or sectoral lending may be an effective way to tackle certian problems common among the Arab countries. Another advantage for policy coordination can be found in country lending schemes (e.g., coordinated country lending to various key Arab countries such as Egypt or the Sudan). This coordination of country lending would prove beneficial for the donors (by avoiding duplication and waste of resources) and for the recipients (by integrating aid in a meaningful way for a maximum effect on the country's economy).

The two levels of coordination among the Arab funds (the technical level and the policy, decision-making level) can be implemented separately. As a first stage, the technical coordination as perceived in the proposed Joint

Technical Services Center may be easier to achieve and would face less obstacles than coordination on the decision-making level. Technical coordination requires that each of the funds devote some of its financial resources and technical personnel for service in the center. It is obvious that some of the funds would be able to devote more resources to this center than others, and some would accrue more benefits than others from joint technical collaboration. But technical cooperation should not create many frictions or areas of conflict because it does not interfere with the authority structure or the decision-making processes in the various funds. Rather, it results in a service and it does not require each of the funds to relinquish or limit its freedom in decision making

At another and higher stage of cooperation, there is the policy and decision-making coordination among the various funds. At that level each of the funds, in the process of arriving at policy coordination in such areas as program or country lending, would have to relinquish some of its autonomy in making policy decisions for the sake of successful coordination. Also in coordinating the funds' work at routine points of contact (e.g., sending joint evaluation missions or negotiating teams, harmonizing project identification and selection practices, establishing uniform disbursement practices), a certain degree of autonomy in decision making would have to be foregone for the sake of establishing new mechanisms for coordination.

Any proposal for establishing coordination mechanisms among the funds may be rendered impractical by certain hazards that presently exist or that may develop later. Such hazards include competition among the various funds for prestige or relevance, parochial perception by the various leaderships of their institutional interests, to the detriment of the more general and regional interests, the hazard of getting paralyzed by intraorganizational conflicts, and the most dangerous of all, cynicism. It may result in the lack of trust in the ability of the various funds to work harmoniously in order to achieve their limited goals in Arab regional development.(33)

The attempts at project cooperation have been going on in the Arab region for some time and have gained momentum with the increase in the financial resources in the region after 1973. Such attempts constitute a promising start for a regional strategy. But, as mentioned earlier, such attempts should not constitute an end-state for regional development. Rather, their value is to provide a base on which to plan and build a more solid and comprehensive regional strategy. The availability of financial resources within the region, the potentialities to increase both agricultural and industrial productions regionally, and the possibility of chronic world-wide shortages of essential commodities in coming years should make the case for an Arab regional strategy a strong one.

Many institutions in the Arab region study and advise policy makers on matters relating to Arab economic development. At a meeting in Cairo in June 1975, the Council for Arab Economic Unity (CAEU) pledged a five-year effort at coordinating the policies of the Arab governments, with the aim of initiating a Middle East Economic Community by 1981.(34) Such an approach recognizes, implicitly, that the Arab Common Market has not been successful as a vehicle for regional development and that liberalization of trade is not the proper avenue for regional development. What seems to be evolving in the Arab region is an emphasis on project and, one hopes, on program or sectoral lending. This is performed on a small scale by the Arab funds covered in this study. However, the resources invested by these funds constitute a very small portion of the total investments in the region and would seem minuscule compared with the total investment potential in the region, in view of the volume of revenues.

The elements of a future strategy for Arab regional development would revolve around investment as the key factor and planning as the effective method. An indication of such a strategy was mentioned earlier in terms of large-scale program lending to tackle certain sectors on a pan-Arab scale (i.e., food production, transportation, small industries network, etc.). In order to gain the support of various policy-makers (or elites, in the strict sociological sense), any regional strategy, however, should not promise only long-term benefits.(35) We have seen that one of the serious problems of economic integration schemes is that their benefits lie ahead in the future. This weakens government support for such schemes.

The difficulties surrounding the evolution of an Arab regional strategy based on integral investment planning would be greater in the initial stages. A balance of interests in the short-run has to be devised. The oil countries would seek immediate returns for their capital invested, while countries with idle or underutilized capacities (Egypt, Syria, the Sudan, Lebanon, etc.) would advocate a long-term perspective for evaluating regional strategies. Invest-ments in productive sectors require gestation periods, and success is not guaranteed. Even adequate planning is not a full guarantee. It was observed that the efficiency of the capitalist system is built on an unending run of bankruptcies of the inefficient firms, so it is hypocritical to expect that planning by central or governmental authorities will be characterized by a utopian run of total success.(36)

This dilemma, which faces any Arab regional strategy, has to be recognized and tackled. The success of projects and programs presently financed by the various Arab funds may create the confidence required to sustain a regional strategy based on planned regional investments, at least for the duration of the difficult initial stages.

THE ARAB FUNDS AND THE UNITED NATIONS SYSTEM

The United Nations system is pursuing policies of assisting institutions seeking to promote regional cooperation in developing countries. This is one aspect among several others signifying the increasing involvement of the United Nations system in problems of economic and social development on national, regional, and global levels.

The United Nations offers a resource pool of expertise and experiences to all developing countries. The United Nations Development Program (UNDP) and the U.N. Conference on Trade and Development (UNCTAD) are increasing their work in economic cooperation among developing countries. In its efforts to promote economic cooperation among developing countries, UNCTAD realized that "emphasis should be shifted decisively from trade matters toward joint endeavours in the development of regional industrial and agricultural resources."(37) As discussed earlier, the Arab countries share similar views. By virtue of its ability to pool technical and financial resources for the service of regional development and cooperation, the United Nations helps to promote those same goals in the Arab region.

The role of the United Nations in economic cooperation and development in the Arab region ranges from the general to the specific.

In general, the United Nations system articulates the interests of developing countries on a global level and provides the mechanism through which such interests are translated into operational activities. The United Nations has sponsored conferences and studies on ways to strengthen cooperation among developing countries. Efforts to promote self-reliance on national and regional levels among developing countries are also being pursued. A Conference on Economic Cooperation Among Developing Countries was held under United Nations auspices in Mexico City in September 1976. Conference on Technical Cooperation Among Developing Countries (TCDC) was convened in 1978, and a conference on science and technology for development is being arranged for 1979. The Arab region, among other developing regions, is bound to benefit from these conferences both as a contributor and recipient of ideas and suggestions.

On a specific level, certain agreements were reached between United Nations organs and Arab institutions. These agreements spell out specific goals of economic cooperation and regional development. The work of the Economic Commission for Western Asia (ECWA) and the agreement between UNDP and the Arab Fund to promote intercountry projects are two specific examples of the contributions of the UN system to Arab regional development.

The Economic Commission for Western Asia (ECWA) was established in January 1974 to replace the United Nations Economic and Social Office in Beirut. Its creation marked the beginning of a new era of cooperation between the United Nations and the Arab countries in economic and social development. ECWA was designed to combine the expertise of the United Nations system with the financial resources of the Arab countries of western Asia in the pursuit of regional development and cooperation.

One of the first and major tasks of ECWA was to coordinate its work with the development finance institutions discussed in this study (viz. AFESD, the Kuwait, Abu Dhabi, and Saudi funds). In 1974, regular and periodical meetings were scheduled to coordinate the work among the Arab funds and ECWA. Issues related to regional economic cooperation were discussed, with the view of promoting projects geared toward regional development. Regional cooperation at the micro (project) level was perceived to play the role of catalyst for a broader concept of cooperation in the region.(38)

The Arab funds decided to support ECWA in creating a data bank for the economic and social sectors of the Arab countries, including those countries outside the western Asia region. The Arab development funds also agreed to finance an ECWA program to recruit experts to help the Arab countries identify and prepare development projects.(39)

The civil war in Lebanon, however, had a negative effect on ECWA's performance. Late in 1976, it was decided that the temporary headquarters of ECWA be transferred to Amman and that the permanent headquarters be established in Baghdad. The improvement of the situation in Lebanon and the decisions in regard to ECWA's headquarters are expected to enable the ECWA secretariat to resume its normal functions once again.

Indeed, there are recent indications that ECWA is trying to compensate for time lost during the past two years. Agreements are sought between ECWA and Arab League development institutions, such as the Council for Arab Economic Unity.(40) ECWA is also trying to respond to regional needs in terms of expanding its geographical covering and its ability to attend to the particular concerns of the Arab world. During its fourth session, in Amman, in April 1977, ECWA recommended to the Economic and Social Council of the United Nations the acceptance of Egypt (presently a member of the Economic Commission for Africa) and the Palestine Liberation Organization as full members of ECWA.(41)

The agreement between AFESD and UNDP for the promotion of intercountry and integration projects is another specific example of the United Nations role in promoting Arab economic cooperation. The agreement was signed on December 28, 1975, between the Arab Fund, UNDP and representatives of Arab-government members of the Arab Fund.(42) The program calls for contributions from the Arab Fund ($9,396,000), the UNDP ($6,268,000), and Arab governments ($3,500,000) to identify and prepare intercountry investment projects. The duration of the agreement is six years, during which the Arab Fund would be the executing agency for UNDP.

This program was inspired, to a great extent, by the results of a joint ECWA/UNIDO (United Nations Industrial Development Organization) Meeting on Special Problems and Requirements of Industrial Development in Selected Countries of the Middle East, held in Beirut in November 1974. The meeting identified two avenues for promoting project cooperation among Arab countries.   The first is through close cooperation between technical assistance organizations and financial institutions, particularly in connection with preinvestment work. The second is to encourage financing institutions to dedicate a larger proportion of their resources to technical assistance.

The joint program between AFESD and UNDP tries to meet these two recommendations as a means to promote intercountry development projects. The program defines an intercountry project to include a) projects physically located in two or more countries, and b) projects located in one country but of significant economic interest to two or more countries.(43)

The time plan for executing the program calls for the achievement of two tasks: project identification and preparation, and the preparation of feasibility studies for some specific projects to be selected from among the projects identified. The first task calls for the technical cooperation among the Arab Fund, the Council on Arab Economic Unity (CAEU), UNDP, UNCTAD, UNIDO, etc. The second task will be mainly the responsibility of the Arab Fund.

One of the first subordinate tasks is to prepare a manual for the identification, preparation, and evaluation of intercountry investment projects. In 1977, UNCTAD consultants prepared such a manual for discussion in an expert group meeting.(44) In view of our earlier description, there is reason to believe that numerous opportunities exist in the Arab region for the development of integration (or multicountry) projects. One such opportunity, which has already been explored, is the Basic Program for Agriculture Development in the Sudan, mentioned in Chapter 3.

Integration or intercountry projects usually result in the use of idle capacity. This is true in the case of the Sudan-Arab Fund program. The same applies to industrial production in the Arab region. Some Egyptian industries, for example, provide the opportunity for integration projects based on the use of existing underutilized industrial capacities. Moreover, the widening of markets implicit in integration or intercountry projects provides for the exploitation of the advantages associated with specialization. An example of benefits apparently foreclosed is the duplication of petrochemical industries in the Arab Gulf countries. An integration project that meets the needs of these countries and utilizes the special advantages associated with the oil production in the area would avoid the waste of resources implicit in the duplication of such water-intensive industries.

The numerous development institutions in the Arab region could also count on the support of the United Nations specialized agencies, such as the Food and Agriculture Organization (FAO) and World Health Organization (WHO), to provide technical expertise in their respective fields.(45) An example of increased cooperation between the Arab funds and United Nations bodies could be found in the number of projects confinanced by the World Bank group and the Arab funds. In 1974, only three projects were cofinanced by the World Bank and OPEC bilateral aid organizations (including the three funds covered in this study), but by 1976 the number of such cofinanced projects had increased to 26.(46) This collaboration joins the World Bank's experience in the technical aspects of project lending with the Arab funds' increased financial capabilities and growing technical experience. However, the Arab funds perceive the World Bank processing of loan applications to be slow and consider many of the bank's procurement policies to be inflexible. Such a situation probably impedes greater collaboration between the bank and the Arab lending institutions.

At this juncture, the stakes are high, where Arab regional development is concerned. As UNDP rightly remarked:

> From a regional perspective, one can perceive the Arab world today with a highly skewed distribution of differing and complementary resources – skilled and unskilled human resources, rich and poor in capital, an abundance and absence of natural resources – with its major natural resource being rapidly depleted; its capital subject to erosion; and with the necessity of a dramatic economic transformation within a generation.(47)

Such an obvious need for an economic transformation should lead Arab policy makers to realize the high risks involved in missing the present opportunity for regional development. With such realization, common actions in the economic field could be forthcoming as mentioned above, there is a community of interests and aspirations in the Arab region. When a danger is perceived to threaten this community, the Arabs join forces in order to preserve their interests. It has been observed that if the Arab oil-producing countries, in particular, "fail to adopt adequate development policies . . . (they may end up) . . . in a situation worse, from the social as well as the human point of view, than before the oil era."(48)

For both oil- and nonoil-producing Arab countries, the present opportunity for economic cooperation and regional development should not be missed. The loss of such an opportunity would probably have grave consequences for both groups.

Summary and Conclusions

In this study, three Arab development funds were surveyed. We analyzed their organizational dynamics and policy orientations. Our purpose has been to identify areas of existing and potential cooperation among the funds and between them and the organizations of the United Nations system. Such cooperation was conceived in the context of Arab regional development.

This study discussed the similar problems the funds face along the path toward achieving their common goals of Arab regional development. These problems emanate, inter alia, from the tremendous tasks the funds hope to achieve. Some of the problems relate to aspects that cannot be changed except in the long run (e.g., shortage in professional staff); others are amenable to immediate policy manipulation (e.g., a coordination mechanism to avoid duplication of activities). The three funds studied here, however, constitute one part of a larger arena of development aid institutions created in the past few years by oil-exporting developing countries. The Saudi and Iraqui funds, the Islamic fund, the Arab Bank for Economic Development in Africa, and the OPEC Special Fund are not covered in this study (mainly because they are much more recent which makes comparison of data and appraisal of work more difficult). Their contributions, however, are worthy of other future studies.

We have noted that the achievements of the three Arab funds in project and program cooperation might offer a successful base upon which to build a more ambitious and far-reaching regional development strategy. With the increase in oil revenues in the region, a more integrated picture of economic complementarities is becoming apparent. Some countries are rich in capital, others in human resources, still others in unutilized or underutilized agricultural and mineral resources. This picture calls for a regional development strategy based on region-wide investment planning, yet to be achieved.

In this work we discussed the process by which the funds could be a focal point for elaborating a strategy for regional investment planning. We indicated that in order to spearhead a new regional strategy based on tackling development-financing problems on a regional basis, the funds would have to achieve a coordination mechanism on both the technical and policy levels. Technical coordination among the funds is under discussion via the proposed Joint Technical Services Center. The more ambitious policy-coordination step is undoubtedly shrouded in political uncertainties.

The role of the United Nations system in promoting Arab regional development revolves mainly, in this study, around the ECWA and UNDP regional efforts, in which the Arab funds assume an important function. The role of the World Bank group is also linked with the various Arab funds through cofinancing. Therefore we posit that higher degrees of coordination among the funds would further facilitate the United Nations efforts in promoting Arab regional development. Such would be the case because cooperation among the funds (represented as one coordinated system) and the United Nations bodies could be planned on a regional scale rather than on a country basis, depending on the priorities established by each fund separately. In this way, cooperation with the United Nations bodies involved in Arab regional development would be enhanced for the ultimate benefit of the people in the region.

Appendix A
The Kuwait Fund
For Arab
Economic Development:
Law and Charter

Law No. 25 (1974) Level 1
for the Reorganization of the Kuwait Fund
for Arab Economic Development

We, Jaber Al-Ahmed Al-Jaber, Al-Sabah, Deputy Amir and Crown Prince of the State of Kuwait.

Having considered Article 61 and Article 65 of the Constitution:

And Law No. 35 (1961) for the Establishment of the Kuwait Fund for Arab Economic Development, as amended by Law No. 9 (1963) and Law No. 64 (1966):

Hereby assent to and enact the Law passed by the National Assembly and set forth herein below:

Article 1

The Kuwait Fund for Arab Economic Development, hereinafter called the Fund, shall be a public corporation with an independent legal personality under the supervision of the Prime Minister who shall be the Chairman of the Board of Directors.

Article 2

The purpose of the Fund is to assist Arab States and Developing States in developing their economies and, in particular, to provide such States with loans for the implementation of their development programmes, in accordance with the provisions of a Charter to be made by Order of the Prime Minister.

Article 3

(a) The capital of the Fund shall be one thousand million Kuwaiti Dinars.

(b) An amount of four hundred million Kuwaiti Dinars of the said capital shall be paid out of Government reserves by transfers made from time to time according to the needs of the Fund.

(c) The remaining part of the Fund's capital amounting to six hundred million Kuwaiti Dinars shall be paid out of the public revenues of the State by the appropriation of a percentage of the said revenues annually.

The Law enacting the State Budget shall determine in each year the percentage of public revenues to be appropriated for payment of the aforesaid part of the capital.

Article 4

The Fund may borrow and issue bonds subject to the limit of twice the amount of its capital and reserves in accordance with such terms and conditions as may be determined by the Prime Minister upon the recommendation of the Board of Directors.

Article 5

The Fund shall be administered by a Board of Directors in accordance with the Charter.

Article 6

The Prime Minister shall lay down the Charter of the Fund, which shall in particular, provide for the composition of the Board of Directors and its functions, regulate the technical and administrative work of the Fund and the manner of preparing its budget; and prescribe such other procedures as may be necessary for the proper conduct of the affairs of the Fund.

Article 7

The Prime Minister may delegate all or part of his powers under this law to the Minister of Finance and Oil.*

Article 8

Law No. 35 (1961) for the Establishment of the Kuwait Fund for Arab Economic Development is hereby repealed. However, all Orders made for its implementation not in conflict with the provisions of this Law shall remain in force until superseded by new orders.

---

*Wherever reference is made to "The Minister of Finance and Oil" in the Fund's Law or Charter, it should now read "the Minister of Finance."

Article 9

The Prime Minister and the Minister of Finance and Oil shall implement this Law which shall take effect from the date of its publication in the Official Gazette.

Deputy Amir of the State of Kuwait
Jaber Al-Ahmed Al-Jaber Al-Sabah

Given at Al-Sif Palace on 27 Jumada Al-Thani 1394 A.H. corresponding to July 17, 1974 A.D.

Order of the Prime Minister for the Implementation of Law No. 25 (1974) for the Reorganization of the Kuwait Fund for Arab Economic Development

The Prime Minister,

Having considered Law No. 25 (1975) for the Reorganization of the Kuwait Fund for Arab Economic Development, Hereby makes the following Order:

Article 1

The Kuwait Fund for Arab economic Development shall operate in accordance with the provisions of the Charter attached hereto.

Article 2

The Order of the Minister of Finance and Oil laying down the Charter for the Kuwait Fund for Arab economic Development and published in the Official Gazette No. 423 dated April 14, 1963, is hereby repealed.

Article 3

The Board of Directors of the Kuwait Fund for Arab Economic Development shall implement this Order which shall take effect from the date of its publication in the Official Gazette.

Prime Minister

Given on 2nd Dhul Hijjah, 1394 A.H.
corresponding to December 22, 1974 A.D.

Charter of the Kuwait Fund for Arab Economic Development

Chapter One
General Provisions

Article 1

The Kuwait Fund for Arab Economic Development, hereinafter called the Fund, is a Kuwaiti Public Corporation with an independent legal personality as well as financial and administrative autonomy under the supervision of the Prime Minister who shall be the Chairman of its Board of Directors.

Article 2

The purpose of the Fund is to assist Arab and other developing States in developing their economies and, in particular, to provide such States with loans for the implementation of their development programmes, in accordance with the provisions of this Charter.

Article 3

The capital of the Fund is one thousand million Kuwaiti Dinars.

Article 4

The principal office of the Fund shall be located in the City of Kuwait.

Chapter Two
The Administration of the Fund

Article 5

The Fund shall be administered by a Board of Directors composed of the Prime Minister, as Chairman, and eight other Kuwaiti members of recognized competence appointed by the Prime Minister for a term of two years subject to renewal.

In the event that the office of a member shall become vacant, a new member shall be appointed to hold office for the remainder of the term of his predecessor.

The Director-General of the Fund shall attend the meetings of the Board of Directors and participate in its deliberations but shall not be entitled to vote.

The Chairman may designate a member of the Board of Directors to preside over a meeting of the Board of Directors in his absence.

Article 6

The Chairman of the Board of Directors shall have the authority to sign agreements whereby the Fund lends or borrows money, as well as any bonds issued by the Fund. The Chairman may delegate such authority to the Director-General.

Article 7

The Board of Directors shall be the highest authority of the Fund. It shall have the power to determine the general policy of the Fund for the achievement of its objectives and shall, in particular, have the power to:

(a) consider the recommendations submitted by the Director-General concerning proposed loans and other forms of assistance to Arab and other developing States and make the appropriate decisions;

(b) determine, subject to the provisions of this Charter, the form and terms for the participation of the Fund in the development projects and programs of Arab and other developing States;

(c) approve the amounts of loans and other types of assistance;

(d) determine the general policy of investments by the Fund and the forms of such investments. The Board of Directors may delegate its powers in this respect to the Director-General;

(e) authorize the borrowings of the Fund and determine the amounts and terms of such borrowings;

(f) lay down administrative and financial regulations for the Fund and supervise their implementation;

(g) approve the proposed administrative budget and the closing account of the Fund;

(h) appoint the Fund auditors and determine their remuneration.

Article 8

The Board of Directors shall hold at least four meetings annually. Meetings shall be held at the invitation of the Chairman or the Director-General. A quorum for any meeting of the Board of Directors shall be a majority of the members.   Unless otherwise provided in this Charter, resolutions of the Board of Directors shall be adopted by a simple majority of the votes of members present. In the event of an equal division of votes, the vote of the Chairman shall be deemed a casting vote.

Article 9

The Board of Directors may from time to time appoint subcommittees from among its members to study such matters as may be referred to them and submit their recommendations to the Board. Each subcommittee shall elect a Chairman from among its members.

Article 10

The resolutions of the Board of Directors approving loans and grants, as well as the administrative budget and the closing account shall be subject to confirmation by the Chairman.

Article 11

The Chairman of the Board of Directors shall appoint the Director-General of the Fund and one or more Deputies upon the recommendation of the Board of Directors. The appointment of other staff of the Fund shall be made in accordance with the staff regulations to be laid down by the Board of Directors.

Article 12

The Director-General shall have the direct responsibility for all administrative, financial, and technical matters in the Fund. He shall represent the Fund before the Courts of Law and in relation to third parties. His functions shall, in particular, including the following:

(a) implementation of the resolutions of the Board of Directors;

(b) preparation and submission to the Board of Directors of the proposed administrative budget and the closing account;

(c) authorization of expenditures within the limits of the administrative budget;

(d) submission of an annual report to the Board of Directors on the progress of work in the Fund; such report shall include financial statements certified by auditors and a detailed account of the activities of the Fund during the preceding financial year;

(e) receipt of applications for loans and financial and technical assistance; appraising such applications and submitting appropriate recommendations thereon to the Board of Directors;

(f) implementation of loan and other agreements for the provision of assistance; and

(g) undertaking such other tasks as may be entrusted to him by the Board of Directors in conformity with the provisions of this Charter.

The Director-General shall be assisted by one or more Deputies in carrying out his duties. The senior Deputy present shall act for the Director-General in his absence.

Chapter Three
Operations of the Fund

Article 13

The Fund may assist Arab and other developing States in implementing development projects and programs by making loans to such states or to corporate entities which are under the control of such states or which are subjects of, or constitute joint ventures among such states, provided that the objectives of such corporate entities are not purely limited to the making of profit. The Fund may also provide assistance by issuing guarantees for the obligations of such states or corporate entities, or through any other means which the Board of Directors may consider appropriate.

Article 14

The Fund may not finance by means of a loan more than 50% of the total costs of any project or program. Notwithstanding this provision, the Board of Directors may, by a majority of two-thirds of the members present, approve loans in amounts exceeding the aforesaid limit in exceptionalcases when the necessary financing for a vital project or program cannot otherwise be obtained on reasonable terms.

Article 15

The loans made by the Fund shall be for the purpose of financing, exclusively, all or part of the foreign exchange costs of projects or programs. However, in exceptional cases where sufficient justification exists, the Fund may, pursuant to a decision of the Board of Directors by a majority of two-thirds of the members present, participate in financing the local component of the cost of such projects or programs.

Article 16

The Kuwaiti dinar shall be the unit of account in all operations of the Fund. All loans and other forms of financial assistance made by the Fund shall be paid and repaid, as the case may be, in Kuwaiti Dinars on the basis of the gold parity of the Dinar as specified in the Special Agreement with the International Monetary Fund at the time of signing the agreement for the loan or other type of financial assistance.

Article 17

Each loan agreement shall provide for the payment to the Fund, in addition to the interest charged, if any, of a service charge of one-half of one percent (0.5%) annually on the amounts withdrawn from the loan and outstanding, to cover administrative expenses and other costs incurred in the execution of the loan agreement.

Article 18

All loan agreements between the Fund and the borrowers shall include the following:

(a) financial clauses specifying the duration allowed and conditions for withdrawal of proceeds of the loan, and the dates and conditions for the repayment of the principal thereof and payment of interest, if any, and other charges on the loan;

(b) an undertaking by the borrower to furnish sufficient information to the Fund on the progress of work on the project financed, starting from the date of signature of the loan agreement until the loan is fully repaid;

(c) an undertaking by the borrower to afford all the necessary facilities to representatives of the Fund to enable them to follow up the progress of the project financed;

(d) provisions setting out arrangements for ensuring that the amounts withdrawn from the loan shall be used exclusively for financing expenditures on the project financed and only as such expenditures are actually incurred;

(e) an undertaking that no other external debt shall have priority over the loan of the Fund or the interest or other charges thereon by way of a lien on the assets of the borrower, except within such limits as the Fund may accept;

(f) an undertaking to exempt all transactions, assets and income of the Fund in the recipient state from all taxes, dues and other impositions;

(g) an undertaking from the monetary or any other competent authority in the recipient state to facilitate all the financial operations of the Fund and, in particular, to lift all foreign exchange restrictions on direct and indirect transfers arising out of the loan agreement;

(h) an undertaking to consider all Fund documents, records, correspondence and similar material, as confidential, and to accord the Fund full immunity from censorship and inspection of printed matters; and

(i) an undertaking to exempt all the assets and income of the Fund from nationalization, confiscation and seizure.

Where the loan is made to an entity other than the recipient state, the undertakings set out in paragraphs (f), (g), (h), and (i) of this Article shall be incorporated in a Guarantee Agreement to be concluded between the Fund and the Government of the State guaranteeing the loan.

Article 19

The Fund may require, depending on the nature of each transaction, additional guarantees other than those provided for in the preceding Article, and may accept guarantees made by third parties including those of national, regional and international financial institutions.

Article 20

In considering loan applications the Fund shall be guided by the recognized principles of development finance including, in particular, the following:

(a) The degree of importance of the project or program for which the loan is requested and its priority rating in relation to other projects or programs;

(b) The completeness and accuracy of the cost estimates for the project or program;

(c) The adequacy of the economic and technical evaluation of the project;

(d) Ascertainment of the availability of the funds necessary, in addition to the financing to be provided by the Fund, for the execution and completion of the project or program;

(e) The solvency of the applicant and the guarantor, if any.

Article 21

All loan agreements between the Fund and the borrowers shall be made in the Arabic language.

Article 22

The Fund shall not make grants to any beneficiaries except against its accumulated net profits.

Article 23

The Fund may borrow money, issue bonds and give guarantees within the limit of twice the amount of its capital and reserves, in accordance with such terms and conditions as may be determined by the Prime Minister upon the recommendation of the Board of Directors.

Chapter Four
Financial Provisions

Article 24

The financial year of the Fund shall begin on the first day of April and end on the last day of March of the following year.

Article 25

The Fund shall have an administrative budget comprising its income and current expenditures and shall prepare a closing account in respect of such income and expenditures. The Director-General shall submit the draft administrative budget to the Board of Directors not later than two months before the end of each financial year.

Article 26

The Fund shall prepare a Balance Sheet, an Income and Expenditure Statement and a Reserve Account. The said financial statements shall be certified by auditors and submitted to the Board of Directors, together with the Closing Account and the Annual Report on the activities of the Fund, not later than June 30 of each year.

Article 27

The Fund shall keep proper books of accounts to show a true and fair view of the state of affairs of the Fund and explain its transactions. The Auditors' report shall be submitted to the Board of Directors for consideration and approval.

Article 28

Without prejudice to the provisions of Article 22 of this Charter, net profits of the Fund shall be credited to a reserve account until reserves shall become equal to twenty percent (20%) of the capital of the Fund. Thereafter, net profits shall be added to the capital of the Fund provided however, that the reserves shall always remain equal to twenty percent of the capital.

Chapter Five
Miscellaneous Provisions

Article 29

The Prime Minister may delegate all or part of his powers under this Charter to the Minister of Finance and Oil.

Article 30

This Charter may be amended by a decision of the Prime Minister upon the recommendation of the Board of Directors.

Appendix B
Agreement Establishing
The Arab Fund for
Economic and
Social Development

Agreement Establishing the Arab Fund for Economic and Social Development

The Governments of: The Hashimite Kingdom of Jordan
The Republic of Tunisia
The Algerian Democratic and People's Republic
The Democratic Republic of the Sudan
The Republic of Iraq
The Kingdom of Saudi Arabia
The Syrian Arab Republic
The Libyan Arab Republic
The Arab Republic of Egypt
The Yemen Arab Republic
The State of Kuwait
The Republic of Lebanon
The Kingdom of Morocco
The People's Democratic Republic of Yemen
The State of The United Arab Emirates
The State of Bahrain
The State of Qatar

Desirous of building the Arab Economy on a strong foundation that will enable it to meet the requirements of economic and social development in their countries, and in order to achieve the aims of the Pact of the League of Arab States.

Have approved the text of this Agreement as adopted by the Economic Council in its resolution Number 345 at its meeting held on Thursday, 18th Safar, 1388 H., (May 16, 1968).

Article 1

There shall be established an Arab regional financial organization, enjoying an independent juridical personality, called the "ARAB FUND FOR ECONOMIC AND SOCIAL DEVELOPMENT," and having its Head Office in the City of Kuwait. The Fund may, by a decision of the Board of Governors as provided for in Article 19, establish branches and agencies in any country.

PART ONE
Purposes of the Fund

Article 2

The Fund shall participate in the financing of economic and social development projects in the Arab states and countries by:

1 – Financing economic projects of an investment character by means of loans granted on easy terms to Governments, and to public or private organizations and institutions, giving preference to economic projects that are vital to the Arab entity and to joint Arab projects.

2 – Encouraging, directly or indirectly, the investment of public and private capital in such a manner as to ensure the development and growth of the Arab economy.

3 – Providing technical expertise and assistance in the various fields of economic development.

PART TWO
Membership and Capital

Article 3

1 – Member States of the League of Arab States and other Arab countries having subscribed to the capital of the Fund before the 1st of July 1968. These shall be considered as founding members.

2 – Any other Arab states or countries whose accession to the Agreement shall be approved by the Board of Governors.

Article 4

The Board of Governors of the Fund may decide to accept the participation of public and private Arab financial institutions and organizations in the Arab states and countries in the capital of the Fund.

Article 5

1 – The capital of this Fund shall be One Hundred Million Kuwaiti dinars (one Kuwaiti dinar being equal to 2.48828 grams of gold) that are convertible into convertible currencies.

2 – The capital shall be divided into ten thousand shares having a value of ten thousand Kuwaiti dinars each.*

3 – Upon signing this Agreement, the founding members shall subscribe shares of the capital of the Fund in accordance with the following schedule. (Deleted; see Table 3.1.)

Article 6
Increase of Capital

The capital of the Fund may be increased on the following conditions:

1 – The approval by an absolute majority of the votes cast in the case of issuing new shares for allocation to an Arab country wishing to join the Fund.

2 – The approval by a three-fourths majority of the votes cast in all other cases.

3 – In case an increase is decided upon pursuant to the preceding paragraph, every member may subscribe thereto in the proportion which its shares bear to the capital and under such conditions as the Board of Governors may decide. This proportion may be increased or reduced, subject to the approval of an absolute majority of the votes cast.

4 – Only members of the Fund and institutions and organizations provided for in Article 4 hereof, can subscribe for shares in an increase of capital;

Article 7
Subscription

1 – Each founding member shall subscribe shares in accordance with the schedule set forth in paragraph 3 of Article 5. The Board of Governors shall determine the shares to be subscribed by other members in the manner provided for in paragraph 1 of Article 6.

2 – Shares shall be issued at their nominal value.

3 – The member shall pay 10% of the value of the shares for which it has subscribed upon depositing the instruments of ratification of this Agreement. The member shall deposit such amount in the Fund's name with the Ministry of Finance of the State of Kuwait, which shall invest it under Government guarantee and return it together with the profits accruing therefrom to the body that the Board of Governors of the Fund shall designate at its first meeting.

---

*The capital of the Fund has become 102,050,000 Kuwaiti dinars with the issuance of 200 new shares to cover the subscription of the Sultanate of Oman and 5 shares to cover the subscription of Palestine.

4 – In addition to the stipulations in paragraph 3, the member shall pay 10% of the value of the shares for which it has subscribed, upon this Agreement coming into force, pursuant to Article 40 hereof.

5 – The remaining capital shall be paid up in ten equal annual installments, the first of which shall fall due one year after the Fund shall commence its operations.

6 – In case of accession of an Arab state or country to this Agreement after its coming into force, the new member shall pay on the share portion allotted to it, an amount proportionately equal to that paid by existing members of their shares.

Article 8

1 – No member shall be deemed liable, by virtue of its membership, for the Fund's obligations beyond the limits set out in this Agreement.

2 – Every member shall remain liable for the unpaid portion of its shares.

3 – The provisions of paragraphs 1 and 2 of this Article shall apply to the organizations and institutions provided for in Article 4.

Article 9
Disposal of Shares

Shares in the Fund may not be disposed of in any manner whatsoever, nor may their title be transferred, except to the Fund.

Article 10
Resources of the Fund

1 – The Fund's resources shall consist of the capital subscribed, the reserves, and the loans raised by the Fund through the issuing of bonds or the obtaining of credits from public and private Arab institutions or from individuals or international institutions.

2 – The Fund shall determine the conditions relating to bonds issue.

3 – The value of the bonds issued by the Fund may not, at any time, exceed twice the amount of the capital, unless by special resolution of the Fund's Board of Governors to be adopted by a two-third majority of votes.

PART THREE
Functions of the Fund

Article 11
Operations of the Fund

The Fund shall, in particular, carry out the following operations:

1 – Borrow funds from internal and foreign markets and determine the guarantee necessary therefor.

2 – Guarantee the securities relating to the projects wherein the Fund has invested its resources in order to facilitate their sale.

3 – Buy and sell the securities issued or guaranteed by it or wherein it has invested its resources.

4 – Invest surplus resources, its savings and pension funds and the like, in first class securities.

5 – Carry out any other operation connected with the purposes of the Fund as provided for in Article 2.

Article 12
Guarantees

1 – All lending operations undertaken by the Fund in favour of a public or private organization or institution shall be guaranteed by the Government of the State or the country where the project is carried out.

2 – The Fund is entitled, when financing a non-governmental project, to ask for special guarantees in addition to the governmental guarantees stipulated in paragraph 1 of this Article.

Article 13
Limitations on Financing

1 – The Fund shall not finance a project in the territory of any member without the permission of the government concerned.

2 – The Fund shall stipulate that the proceeds of the loan be used for the purposes for which the loan was granted.

3 – The Fund shall not share in the management of any project wherein it has invested its resources.

4 – The Fund shall carry out its financing operations on the terms it shall deem appropriate, taking into consideration the requirements and risks of the project.

5 – The Fund shall ascertain, through its technical experts, the viability of any project before financing it.

6 – The Fund shall strive for the continuous investment of its resources on satisfactory terms.

7 – The Fund may raise loans in any member country to finance a project after obtaining the permission of the government of that country. In case the project is to be carried out in the country of another member, the member in whose country the loan is raised shall undertake to transfer the proceeds of the loan to the country where the project is to be carried out, at the Fund's request.

Article 14
Currencies in which
loans are granted

The Fund shall pay the borrower the amount of the loan in the currency agreed upon by the two parties as required for the execution of the project.

Article 15
Conversion of Currencies

The Fund shall be entitled to convert the currencies at its disposal into any other currency deemed best suited for its purposes.

Article 16
Repayment of Loans

Contracts relating to the loans granted by the Fund shall provide for the methods of repayment of such loans as follows:

1 – The Fund shall determine the cost of the loans granted by it, the commission, the methods of discharge of the debt, the dates of maturity, the payment, and the conditions relating thereto.

2 – The loan contract shall stipulate the currency in which payments due shall be made. The Fund shall endeavour, as far as possible, to recover its loans in the currency in which they were contracted. The borrower may, however, repay the loan in another currency subject to the approval of the Fund.

3 – The Fund may modify the terms of the loan contract at the borrower's request, but without prejudice to the interest of the Fund or other members and subject to the approval of the guaranteeing government.

4 – The Fund may modify the conditions of repayment of the loan.

Article 17
Prohibition of Political Activity

The Fund and the officers in charge of its management shall not interfere in political affairs. Economic and social considerations shall be the only relevant factors in the making of decisions.

PART FOUR
Organization and Management

Article 18
Structure of the Fund

The Fund shall be composed of the Board of Governors, the Director-General Chairman of the Board of Directors, the Board of Directors, the Loan Committees, and the staff necessary to perform the duties determined by the Administration of the Fund.

Article 19
Board of Governors

1 – The Board of Governors shall consist of a Governor and an Alternate Governor, appointed by each member of the Fund for a period of five years, unless the member considers the replacement of either of them during the said period; they may be reappointed. The Board shall elect every year one of the Governors as its Chairman.

2 – The Board of Governors shall be considered as the General Assembly of the Fund, and shall have all powers. It may delegate to the Board of Directors any of its powers, except the power to:

a – Admit new members.

b – Increase the capital.

c – Suspend a member.

d – Settle disputes over the interpretation of the provisions of this Agreement.

e – Conclude agreements for the purpose of cooperating with other international organizations.

f – Terminate the operations of the Fund and liquidate its assets.

g – Determine the distribution of the net income of the Fund.

3 – The Board of Governors shall meet once a year at least. It shall also meet whenever so requested by any three of its members having one quarter of the

total voting power, or by the Board of Directors.

4 – The meeting of the Board shall be valid provided a quorum is present representing no less than two-third of the total voting power.

5 – The Board of Governors may establish the necessary procedure whereby the Board of Directors may obtain the approval of the members of the Board of Governors on a specific question without calling a meeting of the latter.

6 – The Board of Governors and the Board of Directors, each within its province, may lay down such rules, instructions and regulations as may be necessary to conduct the business of the Fund.

7 – The Governors and their Alternates shall carry out their duties as members of the Board of Governors without remuneration. The Fund, however, shall pay them appropriate expenses incurred in attending meetings.

8 – The Board of Governors shall determine the remuneration to be paid to the members of the Board of Directors and their Alternates, as well as the salary and terms of the contract of service of the Director-General Chairman of the Board of Directors.

Article 20
Voting

1 – For voting purposes at meetings of the Board of Governors, each member shall have two hundred votes, regardless of the number of shares it may hold, plus one additional vote for each share held.

2 – Except as otherwise provided, all matters before the Board shall be decided by an absolute majority of votes.

Article 21
Director-General Chairman of
the Board of Directors and Staff

1 – The Board of Governors shall appoint a Director-General to the Fund who is not a Governor or his Alternate, nor a Director or his Alternate. In case of a temporary absence of the Director-General, the Board of Governors shall appoint a replacement for him to act on his behalf during his absence.

2 – The Director-General shall preside at the meetings of the Board of Directors. He shall have no vote, save in the event of an equal division, in which case he shall have a casting vote. He may be called to attend the meetings of the Board of Governors and take part in its discussions, but shall not vote at such meetings.

3 – The Director-General shall be the head of the staff of the Fund and shall be responsible for conducting all business under the supervision of the Board of Directors. He shall apply technical and administrative regulations within

the Fund, and have the right to appoint and dismiss experts and staff in accordance with the regulations of the Fund.

4 – The Director-General and staff owe their duty to the Fund. In the course of the conduct of business, they must not allow themselves to be influenced by any considerations other than the interest of the Fund, and they shall remain impartial in the discharge of their duties.

5 – In appointing the staff, the Director-General shall pay due regard that positions be distributed to the extent possible amongst nationals of the Arab states and countries members of the Fund, provided that there shall be no departure from the principle of securing the required efficiency and expertise.

Article 22

Board of Directors

1 – The Board of Directors shall be charged with all the activities of the Fund in a general manner, and shall exercise the powers delegated to it by the Board of Governors.

2 – The Board of Directors shall be composed of four full-time Directors elected by the Board of Governors from among Arab citizens of recognized experience and competence. They shall be elected for a term of two years renewable.*

3 – Members of the Board of Directors shall be elected as follows:

a – Each Governor shall nominate as candidates one Director and one Alternate Director.

b – The Board of Governors shall elect from among the candidates four Directors and four Alternate Directors, by a majority of votes.*

c – Each Governor shall delegate to one of the elected Directors the number of votes he represents in the Board of Governors.

4 – The Alternate Directors shall assist the Directors in their work and shall attend the meetings of the Board of Directors. An Alternate Director shall have the right to vote in the absence of the Director for whom he is acting.

5 – The Directors and their Alternates shall continue in office until their successors are appointed. If the office of one of them becomes vacant for a maximum period of ninety days, the Governors whose votes were represented by the former Director shall select a successor for the remainder of the term, provided that such selection is approved by the Board of Governors. The successor shall be in the same position as his predecessor with respect to the number of votes which he represents.

---

*The number of Directors has been increased to six (1977).

6 — Meetings of the Board of Directors shall be valid provided a quorum of two-thirds of the total votes is present.

7 — Resolutions of the Board of Directors shall be adopted by an absolute majority of the votes cast unless otherwise provided.

Article 23
Loan Committees

1 — Loan committees shall be formed to submit the necessary reports on the projects and the adequacy of the loans requested therefor.

2 — Each committee shall include an expert selected by the Governor representing the member in whose territory the project is located, and one or more members of the technical staff of the Fund appointed by the Chairman of the Board of Directors.

Article 24
Reports and Statements

The Fund shall issue an annual general report on its financial position. It may also issue a report on its activities with respect to the various projects as well as any other reports on the carrying out of its purposes. Such reports and statements shall be distributed to all members.

Article 25
Allocation of Net Income

A 10% of the annual net income of the Fund shall be allocated to the General Reserve. The Board of Governors may decide to allocate an additional amount to form a supplementary reserve. The balance shall be distributed to members in proportion to the number of shares held by them.

Article 26
Withdrawal of Members

No member shall have the right to withdraw from the Fund before the expiry of five years of membership. Withdrawal shall be by way of submitting a notice in writing to the Head Office of the Fund, expressing the member's wish to withdraw. Withdrawal shall become effective on the date such notice is received.

Article 27
Suspension of Membership

1 — If a member fails to fulfill any of its obligations to the Fund, its membership may be suspended by decision of a majority of the Board of Governors. The member so suspended shall definitively cease to be a member one year from the date of suspension unless another decision is taken by a majority of votes to readmit the suspended member.

2 – While under suspension a member shall not be entitled to exercise any rights under this Agreement, except the right of withdrawal.

Article 28
Rights and Obligations of
Governments Ceasing to be Members

1 – When a Government ceases to be a member under the provisions of Article 26 and 27, it shall remain liable for all its obligations to the Fund, so long as any part of the loans or guarantees contracted before it ceased to be a member are outstanding; but the former member shall cease to incur any liabilities with respect to new loans or guarantees entered into by the Fund and shall cease to share either in its income or expenses.

2 – When a Government ceases to be a member, the Fund shall purchase the shares of such Government and settle its accounts. The purchase price of the shares shall be the value shown by the books of the Fund or the paid up value, whichever is less.

3 – The payment for shares purchased by the Fund under the preceding Paragraph shall be governed by the following conditions:

a – The Fund shall withhold any amount due to the Government for its shares so long as such Government or any public or private organization or institution in its territory remains liable to the Fund. The Fund shall be entitled to lay hold on the amount withheld in settlement of outstanding loans and obligations. In any event, no amount due to a member shall be paid until at least six months after the date upon which it ceased to be a member.

b – The Fund may pay to the Government for its shares a part of the amount withheld, in proportion to the rights recovered by the Fund.

c – If any loss is sustained by the Fund as a result of the operations undertaken by it under this Agreement and is still outstanding on the date when the Government ceased to be a member, and the amount of the loss exceeds the amount of the reserve provided to be set against such loss on the aforesaid date, then such Government shall be liable to repay upon demand the amount by which the purchase price of the said Government's shares by the Fund would have been reduced if the loss had been taken into account when the purchase price was determined.

Article 29
Suspension of the Operations of
the Fund and Liquidation of its Assets

1 – In an emergency the Board of Directors may temporarily suspend operations in respect of loans, guarantees and participation in projects. It shall convene the Board of Governors to an extraordinary meeting to consider the case and take a decision in this respect.

2 – The Fund may suspend permanently its operations by decision of a majority of three-quarters of the votes of the Board of Governors. The Fund shall, following such a decision, forthwith cease all activities, except such operations and measures as are necessary to the realization, conservation and preservation of its assets and property.

The Fund shall continue to exist, and all mutual rights and obligations between the Fund and its members under this Agreement shall remain standing until the final settlement of its obligations and distribution of its assets. During this time, no member may be suspended, nor may it withdraw, and no assets may be distributed to members except under the provisions of Part Five of this Agreement.

3 – No distribution of the assets of the Fund may be made until all creditors' claims have been settled. Such assets shall be distributed proportionately to the shares held by each member. Distribution shall be effected in cash or other assets at such times and in such currencies as the Fund shall deem appropriate.

4 – Any member receiving assets distributed by the Fund in accordance with the provisions of Part Five shall be subrogated to all the rights pertaining to such assets as the Fund enjoyed prior to their distribution.

PART SIX
Legal Status, Immunities and Privileges

Article 30

1 – The Fund shall possess juridical personality and, in particular, the capacity:

a – to contract;

b – to acquire immovable and movable property and to dispose of same;

c – to institute legal proceedings.

2 – Actions shall be brought against the Fund in the courts having competent jurisdiction in the place where its Head Office is situated, and may be brought against it as well in the place where the dispute has arisen if the Fund has a branch office or an agent authorized to accept notice of process.

3 – No actions shall be brought against the Fund by members or persons acting for or deriving claims from members.

4 – All property and assets of the Fund shall, wherever located and by whomsoever held in the member countries, be immune from all forms of provisional measures before the delivery of final judgment against the Fund.

5 – All property and assets of the Fund, wherever located and by whomsoever held in the member countries, shall be immune from search, requisition, confiscation, expropriation, or any similar forms of compulsory measures by an executive or legislative authority.

6 – The papers, registers and documents of the Fund, wherever located and by whomsoever held, shall be inviolable.

Article 31
Freedom of Assets from Restrictions

All property and assets of the Fund, to the extent necessary to carry out the operations provided for in this Agreement and subject to the provisions of this Agreement, shall be free from all restructions, regulations, controls, and • moratoria of any kind.

Article 32

Communications of the Fund shall be accorded by each member the same treatment that it accords to the official communications of other members.

Article 33
Immunity from Taxation in Member Countries

1 – The Fund, its assets, property, income, its operations and transactions provided for in this Agreement, shall be immune from all taxation and from all custom duties. The Fund shall also be immune from the obligation of collection or payment of any tax or duty.

2 – Shares of the Fund shall be immune from all taxes and duties when issued or circulated.

3 – Bonds and securities issued by the Fund, as well as dividends, interest and commissions thereon and the like, by whomsoever held, shall be immune from taxation of any kind.

Article 34
Immunities and Privileges of Officers
and Employees of the Fund

1 – Governors and their Alternates, Directors and their Alternaties, officers and employees of the Fund shall enjoy the following:

a – Immunity from legal process with respect to acts performed by them in their official capacity;

b – Immunity from immigration restrictions, alien registration requirements and exchange control;

c – Traveling facilities;

d – Immunity from taxation regarding the salaries or remunerations paid to them by the Fund.

2 – In addition to the privileges and immunities accorded to the Fund and its staff under this Agreement, the Board of Governors may determine any other privileges and immunities that it may deem necessary for the achievement of the purposes of the Fund.

Article 35
Amendment of Provisions of the Agreement

1 – Any member, Governor, or Director, shall be entitled to propose amendments to this Agreement, by communicating the amendment proposal to the Chairman of the Board of Governors who shall bring the proposal before the Board at the earliest opportunity. If the proposal is approved by the Board, the Fund shall seek the opinion of all members on same. When three-fourths of the voting members have accepted the proposal, the Fund shall certify the amendment by formal communication addressed to all members. The amendment shall be registered with the Secretariat General.*

2 – Notwithstanding paragraph 1 of this Article, acceptance by all members is required in the case of any amendment modifying:

a – The right to withdraw from the Fund provided in Article 26 hereof;

b – The limitation of the members' liability in respect of the unpaid portion of their shares as provided in Article 8 hereof;

c – An increase of the capital as authorized under paragraph 3 of Article 6 hereof.

3 – Amendments shall come into force for all members three months after the date of the formal communication issued by the Fund, unless a shorter period is fixed by the Board of Governors.

PART SEVEN
Interpretation and Arbitration

Article 36

1 – It shall be within the competence of the Board of Governors to examine and settle all differences arising between any member and the Fund, or between the members themselves, regarding the interpretation of the provisions of this Agreement. The decision of the Board shall be final and binding.

2 – Any member may appeal against the decisions of the Board of Directors

---

*Translator's Note: The "Secretariat General" means the "Secretariat General of the League of Arab States."

interpreting any of the provisions of this Agreement to the Board of Governors who shall give a final and binding decision on the matter in dispute. The Fund, pending the decision of the Board of Governors, may act on the basis of the decision of the Board of Directors.

Article 37
Arbitration

Whenever a disagreement arises between the Fund and a State or a country which has ceased to be a member, or between the Fund and a member during the final liquidation of the Fund, any party may submit such disagreement to arbitration by a tribunal of three arbitrators, one appointed by the Fund, another by the second party, and the third arbitrator shall be selected by the two arbitrators.

In case the two arbitrators fail to agree on the selection of the third arbitrator, the Secretary General of the League of Arab States shall select one from among Arab jurists. The award of the arbitration tribunal shall be final and binding.

PART EIGHT
Final Provisions

Article 38

Every Government shall become member of this Fund as of the date on which it shall deposit with the Secretariat General of the League of Arab States the instruments of ratification or accession.

Article 39
Ratification, Deposit and Accession

1 – This Agreement shall be ratified by the signatory Arab states and countries, in accordance with their basic laws as early as possible. The instruments of ratification shall be deposited with the Secretariat General of the League of Arab States which shall make a record of the depositing of the instruments of ratification and to notify the Arab member states and countries thereof.

2 – Arab states and countries which have not signed this Agreement may accede thereto, following the approval of the Board of Governors, by addressing a notification to the Secretary General of the League of Arab States who shall notify their accession to the Arab states and countries, members of the Fund.

Article 40

This Agreement shall come into force one month after the deposit of the instruments of ratification by states whose total subscription is not less than 45% of the capital stock provided for in Article 5 hereof.

Article 41

The Secretary General of the League of Arab States shall convene the first meeting of the Board of Governors.

IN WITNESS WHEREOF, the authorized delegates whose names appear below have signed this Agreement on behalf and in the name of their Governments.

Done in Cairo, on Thursday, 18th Safar 1388 H., May 16, 1968, in a single document in Arabic to be kept with the Secretariat General of the League of Arab States. A certified true copy shall be handed to each signatory or acceding state.

Appendix C
Abu Dhabi Fund
For Arab
Economic Development:
Laws and Regulations

LAW NO 3 (1971)

ESTABLISHMENT OF THE ABU DHABI FUND
FOR ARAB ECONOMIC DEVELOPMENT

We, Zayed Bin Sultan Al Nehayan, Ruler of Abu Dhabi, in accordance with the proposal of the Prime Minister, as approved by the Council of Ministers, have issued the following Law.

Article 1

A public establishment of independent character, shall be formed in the name of "Abu Dhabi Fund for Arab Economic Development." Its headquarters shall be stationed in Abu Dhabi.

Article 2

The object of the Fund is to offer economic aid to Arab countries in support of their economic development. That is, in the form of loans or participation in projects or guarantees or in other forms that shall be defined by the regulations of the Fund.

Article 3

The capital of the Fund shall be limited by fifty million Bahraini Dinars to be paid by Abu Dhabi Government. The Administrative Board of Directors of the Fund is authorized to apply to the government to pay in, ten million dinars in the first year, and eight million dinars every following year, and that is, according to need, until the full amount of capital is paid in.

Article 4

The Fund may borrow additional money or issue bonds within the limit of double its capital amount and reserves and that is within the stipulations and conditions defined by the Board of Directors of the fund and with guarantee of Abu Dhabi Government.

Article 5

The Fund shall be administered by an Administrative Board presided by the Prime Minister, composed of seven members one of whom shall be Vice-President; and all shall be appointed by a decree, for a period of five years, renewable.

Article 6

The Board of Directors of the Fund is the highest authority in administering actions of the Fund, drawing its policy and shall particularly perform the following:

a) Set the regulations of the Fund.

b) Set the organizational regulations of employment by the Fund.

c) Decide on the applications submitted to the Fund for the obtainment of loans or participations or other than that; and define the conditions for their completion.

d) Determine ways of investment for the Fund's monies.

e) Endorse the Fund's budget before the beginning of the fiscal year, and approves the annual balance sheet and final accounts. That is according to the dates and stipulations defined by the executive regulations.

f) Appoint the auditor to the Fund.

The Board of Directors of the Fund is authorized to entrust part of its powers to the General Manager.

Article 7

The net profits that are realized annually as a result of the activities of the Fund, shall be added to the reserves within the ratios and the stipulations defined by the executive regulations.

Article 8

The Fund shall perform its functions in accordance to the provisions of the temporarily attached provisional regulations and until the Administrative Board of the Fund sets the final regulations.

Article 9

This law should be implemented from the date of its issuance and it shall be published in the official Gazette.

Zayed Bin Sultan Al Nehayan
Ruler of Abu Dhabi

Khalifa Bin Zayed Al Nehayan
Crown Prince and Prime Minister
    Issued on: 22nd Jamad Al Awal 1391
    Accordant: July 15, 1971

INTERNAL REGULATIONS

Abu Dhabi Fund for Arab Economic Development

We, Zayed Bin Sultan Al Nehayan, Ruler of Abu Dhabi,

In accordance with Article 8 of Law No. 3 of 1971, establishing Abu Dhabi Fund for Arab Economic Development

And in accordance with the proposal of the Prime Minister, approved by the Council of Ministers,

Order the promulgation of the following:

Section One
Management of the Fund

Article 1

The Fund shall be administered by a Board headed by the Prime Minister and composed of seven members, one of whom shall be the Vice Chairman. The members shall be appointed by Decree for a period of five years, renewable.

In case the membership of any member ceased, a replacement shall be appointed for the remaining period.

The Vice Chairman shall replace the Chairman in his absence.

Article 2

Chairman of the Board of any one he authorizes, shall be empowered to sign contracts of loans issued, participations, and bonds and contracts of loans raised by the Fund.

Article 3

The Board of Directors of the Fund shall be the highest authority in administering the Fund, and drawing the policy for achieving its purposes. He shall in particular be empowered to undertake the following:

a) Considering and taking decisions concerning applications for loans, participations, and other forms of assistance offered by the Fund.

b) Fixing forms of participation in the projects of Arab States and countries.

c) Approving the volume of loans, participations, and other forms of assistance.

d) Fixing the conditions for participation in projects, within the provisions of these regulations.

e) Determining channels for the investment of monies of the Fund, including purchasing of bonds issued by the borrowers in favor of the Fund, or bonds guaranteed by the Fund, if this became necessary.

f) Fixing the size and conditions of loans raised by the Fund.

g) Drawing up the employment regulations and supervising the implementation thereof.

h) Endorsing the budget and final accounts of the Fund.

i) Delegating such powers to the General Manager as deemed suitable.

Article 4

The Board of Directors of the Fund shall hold six meetings per year, at least, called for by the chairman. The meeting shall form a quorum in presence of a clear majority of the members. Decisions shall be taken by clear majority of the present members.

The Chairman shall have a casting vote, if the votes are equal.

Article 5

The Board of Directors of the fund may form committees as needed for studying specific matters referred by the Board. Recommendations of the committees shall be forwarded to the Board. Each Committee shall elect a reporter of its own members.

Article 6

The General Manager and his deputy shall be appointed by Decree on the recommendation of the Board of Directors. In exception to that, the appointment of the first General Manager, his deputy and the experts, shall be decided by the Government of Abu Dhabi.

Article 7

The General Manager shall be directly responsible for all administrative, financial and technical matter of the Fund. He shall represent the Fund before the Courts and in all relations with other parties. He shall, in particular, be responsible for the following:

a) Carrying out decisions of the Board.

b) Preparing the draft budget for the following year, and forwarding it to the Board of Directors, at least two months before the expiration date of the current fiscal year.

c) Authorizing expenditure in accordance with the budget allocations.

d) Appointing staff of the Fund, keeping provisions of article six in view.

e) Receiving and studying applications for loans and economic assistance, and presentation of same to the Board of Directors.

f) Implementation of loan contracts.

g) Performs all other duties assigned to him by the Board of Directors in accordance with these regulations.

The Deputy General Manager shall assist the General Manager in performing his duties, and shall replace him in his absence.

Article 8

The General Manager shall submit the balance sheet and the final accounts to the Board of Directors not later than two months after the expiration of the fiscal year, together with a report of activities of the Fund, a financial report duly certified by the auditors, and detailed description of the Fund operations during the fiscal year.

Article 9

The General Manager shall attend meetings of the Board, take part in the discussions, but he shall not have a vote.

Section Two
Operations of the Fund

Article 10

The Fund shall participate in Arab projects in the form of loans, participations, guarantees, or any other form prescribed by the Board.

Article 11

Participation of the Fund in any project may not exceed 10% of the capital of the Fund.

Article 12

Participation of the Fund in any project in the form of direct loans, may not exceed 50% of the total cost of that project.

Article 13

In exceptional cases where the Board is convinced that the financing of a vital project cannot be secured on reasonable conditions, the Board, by majority of two thirds of the present members, may decide to forego the provisions of the preceding article.

Article 14

All transactions of the Fund shall be paid and collected in Sterling Pounds based on the gold contents agreed upon with the International Monetary Fund at the date of each contract, or in any other currency prescribed by the Board of Directors.

Article 15

In those exceptional cases where severe difficulties arise in external payments, the Board, by majority of two thirds of members, may decide to temporarily forego the provisions of Article 14.

The Board, after perusal of a detailed report on the balance of external payments of the indebted party submitted by the General Manager, and keeping the financial position of the Fund in view, also may, by majority of two-thirds of members, decide to terminate the duration of exclusion referred to hereabove, or to extend it up to a period of six years.

Article 16

The Fund may participate in Arab projects in currency other than Sterling, if so necessary, provided that the original amount, interest and other expenses are repaid in the same currency prescribed in the loan agreement, calculated on basis of the gold contents prevalent at the date of signature of the contract.

In some exceptional cases, the Board may, by majority of two thrids of the present members, decide that the transfer to the borrower be affected in his local currency.

Article 17

Besides to the interest prescribed in each contract, additional charges amounting to half per cent shall be collected in lieu of administrative expenses and expenses incurred in implementation of the contract.

Article 18

All contracts between the Fund and beneficiary states, shall include the following provisions:

a) Conditions and provisions of drawing the loan, repayment of capital, interest, and other expenses.

b) An undertaking by the beneficiary to provide the Fund with adequate information on the progress of work from the date of signature of the contract until the final settlement of the loan.

c) An undertaking by the beneficiary to provide all facilities necessary for the Fund representatives to inspect and check records of the project, at any time, all duration of the loan.

d) Procedures to ensure that all amounts drawn on account of the loan are utilized for financing the project on account of which the loan had been approved.

e) Exemption of the Fund's assets, properties and income, related to the operations carried out by the Fund in the beneficiary state, from all taxes, and other similar liabilities.

f) An undertaking by the respective monetary authorities in the beneficiary states to facilitate all financial transactions of the Fund, and to exempt it from all restrictions on foreign exchange with regard to direct and indirect transfers relating to the implementation of the loan contract.

g) An undertaking by the beneficiary state to treat all documents, records and correspondences of the Fund, etc. as confidential, and to grant the Fund the right of immunity against control and inspection of its printed materials.

h) An undertaking by the beneficiary state to the effect that the capital and income of the Fund shall not be subject to nationalization, confiscation or sequestration.

Article 19

The Fund may demand other guarantees in addition to those stated in the preceding article, including guarantees by international or regional organizations subject to the nature and circumstances of each operation.

Article 20

The Fund, when considering applications for loans, shall be guided by the following economic considerations:

a) The sound position of the borrower and the guarantor.

b) The soundness and adequacy of financial guarantees submitted by a third party.

c) The relative importance and priority of the project to be financed.

d) Complete and thorough estimate of the cost of project.

e) Thorough economic and technical study of the project, including feasibility study of implementation, if so necessary.

f) Verify that the money required for carrying out and completion of the project, over and above the proportion financed by the Fund, is available.

g) That the project in question does not contradict the economic interest of Abu Dhabi or any other Arab State.

Section Three
General Provisions

Article 21

The Fund shall have a separate budget covering its income and expenditures.

Article 22

The fiscal year of the Fund shall commence on the first of January and expire on the end of December, each year.

The first year shall commence on the date of Law establishing the Fund, i.e., July 15, 1971, and shall expire on the end of December of the same year.

Article 23

The net profits of the Fund shall be added to its reserves fund until this forms 20% of the capital. Thereafter, the net profits shall be added to the capital, provided that the reserve fund shall always form 20% of the capital.

Article 24

The Fund may borrow money, issue bonds and give guarantees not exceeding twice the value of its capital and reserve fund under conditions and circumstances specified by the Board of Directors and with the guarantee of the Government of Abu Dhabi.

Article 25

These regulations shall come into effect as from the date of issue, and shall be published in the Official Gazette.

Signed:

Zayed Bin Sultan Al Nehayan
Ruler of Abu Dhabi

Signed:

Crown Prince and Prime Minister
Khalifa Bin Zayed Al Nehayan
Issued on: 22 Jamad Al Awal 1391 H.
July 15, 1971 A.D.

Amiri Decree No. 31 (1972)

Establishing the Board of Directors of
Abu Dhabi Fund for Arab Economic Development

We, Zayed Bin Sultan Al Nehayan, Ruler of Abu Dhabi,

After perusal of Law No. 3 (1971) establishing Abu Dhabi Fund for Arab Economic Development,

And, in accordance with the proposal of the Prime Minister, approved by the Council of Ministers,

Order the effect of the following:

Article 1

The Board of Directors of Abu Dhabi Fund for Arab Economic Development shall be formed as follows:

Sheikh Khalifa Bin Zayed Al Nehayan: Chairman of the Board

Sheikh Tahnoun Bin Mohammed Al Nehayan

Sheikh Surour Bin Mohammed Al Nehayan

H.E. Ahmed Khalifa Al-Suweidi

H.E. Khalaf Bin Ahmed Al-Itaiba

H.E. Mana's Bin Said Al-Itaiba

H.E. Mohammed Al-Habroush

Dr. Hassan Abbas Zaki

Article 2

Dr. Hassan Abbas Zaki shall be appointed Deputy Chairman of the Board of Directors, and he shall practice powers of the General Manager of the Fund until such a General Manager has been appointed.

Article 3

This decree shall be effective from the date of its promulgation and shall be published in the Official Gazette.

Signed:

Zayed Bin Sultan Al Nehayan
Ruler of Abu Dhabi

Khalifa Bin Zayed Al Nehayan
Prime Minister and Minister
of Defence and Finance
Issued in Abu Dhabi at: 26/6/1392 H
July 8, 1972 A.D.

In the name of God, the Beneficient,
the Merciful

Amiri Decree No. 39
(1971)

We, Zayed Bin Sultan Al Nehayan, Ruler of Abu Dhabi, after perusal of Law No. 3 of 1971 establishing Abu Dhabi Fund for Arab Economic Development, and in accordance with the proposal of the Prime Minister, approved by the Council of Ministers.

Order the effect of the following:

Article 1

Dr. Hassan Abbas Zaki shall be appointed Adviser to the Abu Dhabi Fund.

Article 2

Adviser to the Fund, in agreement with the Chairman of the Administrative Board of the Fund, shall take necessary steps for the establishment of the Fund until the formation of an Administrative Board of the Fund. He shall in particular undertake the following:

a) Lay out rules and regulations governing the operations of the Fund.

b) Draw up the chart of organization of the Fund, and employ staff for its main positions.

c) Hire and prepare suitable premises for the Fund to enable it to function in the required manner.

d) Establish necessary contacts with local and foreign parties according to circumstances, for the purpose of definition of the framework of the Fund, and its introduction to the appropriate international authorities.

Article 3

This decree shall be effective from the date it is published, and shall be published in the Official Gazette.

Signed:

Zayed Bin Sultan Al Nehayan
Ruler of Abu Dhabi

Date: 2/8/1391 H
September 22, 1971 A.D.

Law No. 7 (1974)
Amending Some Provisions of Law No. 3 (1971), Establishing the Abu Dhabi Fund for Arab Economic Development

We, Zayed Bin Sultan Al Nehayan, Ruler of Abu Dhabi,

After having perused the provisions of Law No. 1 (1974) concerning the reorganization of the Government Structure of the Emirate of Abu Dhabi,

And Law No. 2 (1971), concerning the National Advisory Council,

And Law No. 3 (1971), establishing the Abu Dhabi Fund for Arab Economic Development,

And in accordance with the proposal of the Chairman of the Executive Council of the Emirate of Abu Dhabi as approved by the said Council,

Promulgated the following Law:

Article 1

Article 2 of the afore-mentioned Law No. 3 (1971), shall be replaced by the following provisions:

"The purpose of the Fund shall be:

1. to offer economic aid to the Arab countries in support of their economic development, in the form of loans or participation in projects;

2. to offer aid to the African, Asian and other Islamic countries in support of their economic development in the form of loans or participation in projects;

3. to establish or participate in the establishment of financial institutions which complement the purposes of the Fund and help create and foster a financial market in Abu Dhabi;

4. to issue guarantees and other such undertaking specified in the executive regulations to compliment the purposes of the Fund;

5. to employ temporary available liquidity in the various remunerative types of investment;

6. to provide expertise and technical assistance in various fields of economic development;

7. to perform any other activities or services that may be necessary for the realization of the purposes of the Fund."

Article 2

Article 3 of Law No. 3 (1971) shall be replaced by the following provision:

"The authorized capital of the Fund is two thousand million dirhams, totally subscribed for by the Government of Abu Dhabi, and divided into paid-in capital of one thousand million dirhams, and capital on call of one thousand million dirhams.

Two hundred million of the paid-in capital shall be disbursed by the end of 1974, the balance shall be disbursed in four equal annual installments.

The payment of an on call capital shall be made upon the demand of the Board of Directors and according to need."

Article 3

The following new paragraph shall be added to Article 4 of Law No. 3 (1971).

"The Fund may also accept deposits from the Government and public organizations according to the terms and conditions determined by the Board of Directors."

Article 4

This Law shall come into force as of the date of issue and shall be published in the Official Gazette.

Zayed Bin Sultan Al Nehayan
Ruler of Abu Dhabi

Khalifa Bin Zayed Al Nehayan
Crown Prince and President of the
    Executive Board
Issued in Abu Dhabi on:
17th Jamada 2, 1394
July 7, 1974.

Law No. 7 (1975)

IN RESPECT OF AMENDMENTS TO PROVISIONS OF LAW NO. 3 (1971) FOR THE ESTABLISHMENT OF THE ABU DHABI FUND FOR ARAB ECONOMIC DEVELOPMENT

We, Zayed Bin Sultan Al-Nehayan, Ruler of Abu Dhabi,

In consequence of our review to Law No. 1 (1974) in respect of the reorganization of Government structure of the Emirate of Abu Dhabi.

And to Law No. 2 (1971) in respect of the National Advisory Council.

And to Law No. 3 (1971) in respect of the establishment of the Abu Dhabi Fund for Arab Economic Development, and in consideration to the proposal of the Head of the Executive Council of the Emirate of Abu Dhabi as approved by the said Council, have issued the following Law:

Article 1

Article 2 of Law No. 3 (1971), the aforementioned, will be superseded by the following:

The object of the Fund will be confined to the following:

1. Offering Economic Aid to Arab countries in support of its Economic

development, in the form of loans or of participation in projects.

2. Offering Economic Aid to the African, Asian and other Islamic countries in support of its economic development in the form of loans or, of participation in projects.

3. Organizing, or participating in forming Financial Establishments which complement the purpose of the Fund and function to create and support a Financial Market in Abu Dhabi.

4. Issuing guarantees and other such undertakings as specified by the executive table, which complete the purpose of the Fund.

5. Employment of temporary available liquidity in the various rewarding means of investment.

6. Providing experience and technical aids within the various fields of Economic Development.

7. Performing any other activities or services that may be necessary for the realization of the object of the Fund.

Article 2

Article 3 of Law No. 3 (1971) will be superseded by the following:

"Capital allotment allowed to the Fund, will be limited to two thousand million dirhams a sum subscribed in whole by the Government of Abu Dhabi, and divided into two thousand million dirhams, paid and one thousand million as on demand."

Out of the paid capital, 200 million dirhams, will be settled within a period extending to the end of the year 1974; the balance amount will be settled in four equal yearly installments.

The settlement of the Capital amount on demand will be liable to demand of the Board of Directors and according to necessity.

Article 3

A new paragraph will be added to Article 4 of Law No. 3 (1974) as follows:

"The Fund may also accept deposits from the Government and Public Establishments in accordance with the stipulation and circumstances specified by the Board of Directors."

Article 4

Execution of this Law will take effect from the date of its issue, and will be published in the Official Gazette.

KHALIFAH BIN ZAYED AL-NAHAYAN
    Crown Prince and President of the
        Board of Executives

                        ZAYED BIN SULTAN AL NEHAYAN
                            Ruler of Abu Dhabi

Issued in Abu Dhabi
on 17th Jamada 2, 1394
July 7, 1974

Notes and References

INTRODUCTION

(1) A recent study of Arab development funds written in the OECD Development Center emphasized the role the funds could play as financial intermediaries to promote "trilateral" cooperation between capital-rich Arab countries, OECD members and the developing countries of Asia, Africa and Latin America. See Traute Scharf, Arab Development Funds and Banks: Approaches to Trilateral Cooperation. Paris: OECD Development Centre, 1978.

(2) Soliman Demir, The Kuwait Fund and the Political Economy of Arab Regional Development (New York: Praeger, 1976), p. 100.

(3) Abdlatif Al-Hamad, The Middle East Economic Aspirations and the United States (Kuwait: The Kuwait Fund for Arab Economic Development, September 1975), pp. 6-7.

(4) For a recent, articulate, and differing view on the establishment of a new international economic order, see Mahbub Ul Haq, The Poverty Curtain: Choices for the Third World (New York: Columbia University Press, 1976), esp. Part 3, pp. 137-219; Richard N. Cooper, "A New International Economic Order for Mutual Gain," Foreign Policy No. 26 (Spring 1977): 66-102; and Robert L. Rothstein, The Weak in the World of the Strong (New York: Columbia University Press, 1977).

(5) Dankwart A. Rustow and J.F. Mugno, OPEC: Success and Prospects. (New York: New York University Press, 1976), Chapter I.

(6) For detailed figures on OPEC bilateral and multilateral aid, see UNCTAD, Financial Solidarity for Development: Efforts and Institutions of the Members of OPEC (TD/B/627), Sales No. E.77.II.D.4, 1977; OECD, Development Cooperation: 1976 Review (Paris: The Organization of Economic Cooperation and Development, November 1976), pp. 99-125.

(7) Robert E. Asher, "International Agencies and Economic Development: An Overview," International Organization 22 (Winter 1968): 441.

(8) A major element of such a strategy emphasizes joint production ventures. These ventures are gaining increasing significance as a part of cooperation schemes among developing countries along the path toward achieving self-reliance; see Sandro Sideri, "Some Notes on UNCTAD IV," Development and Change 7 (October 1976): 489.

(9) Most of the interviews were structured on the basis of a series of questions submitted to the interviewees before the interview. In many cases, more questions were asked by the interviewer on the basis of the responses given, to clarify or elaborate on certain issues. See L.A. Dexter, Elite and Specialized Interviewing (Evanston, Ill.: Northwestern University Press, 1970).

CHAPTER 1

(1) Robert Stephens, The Arabs' New Frontier (London: Temple Smith, 1973), p. 46.

(2) Fakhry Shehab, "Kuwait: A Super Affluent Society," Foreign Affairs 42 (April 1964): 474.

(3) Charter of the Kuwait Fund for Arab Economic Development, Article (6). The charter was issued in a prime minister order, December 22, 1974. Both the Law No. 25 (1974) for the reorganization of the fund and the charter issued in implementation of the law are published in a Kuwait Fund document: Kuwait Fund for Arab Economic Development: Law and Charter. (Kuwait: The Kuwait Fund for Arab Economic Development, n.d.).

(4) In the discussion of the Kuwait Fund organization we will rely, in part, on our earlier work, Chapters 1 and 2.

(5) Demir, p. 24.

(6) Abdlatif Al-Hamad, The Kuwait Fund (Kuwait: The Kuwait Fund for Arab Economic Development, 1971), p. 18 (in Arabic).

(7) Stephens, p. 49.

(8) Al-Hamad, The Kuwait Fund, p. 17.

(9) The information on the size of the professional staff dates to January 1976. Since then the professional staff has expanded, but we could not offer exact figures.

(10) The term 'bureaucracy' is referred to here in a neutral sense, to indicate its scientific usage, meaning a structure of authority with specific rules for making decisions and handling tasks.

(11) James D. Thompson, Paul B. Hammond, et al., Comparative Studies in Administration (Pittsburgh: University of Pittsburgh Press, 1959), p. 200.

(12) John White, Promotion of Economic Integration Through Development Finance Institutions: Three Case Studies (TAD/EI/MFI/R.2), February, 1974, p. 43.

(13) The political aspects of the fund will be discussed later in this study.

(14) The result of the survey was published in Zakaria A. Nasr and Mohamed W. El-Khoja, Report on Arab Industrial Development Banks (Kuwait: The Kuwait Fund for Arab Economic Development, 1972) (in Arabic).

(15) Abdlatif Al-Hamad, Building up Development-Oriented Institutions in the Arab Countries (Kuwait: the Kuwait Fund for Arab Economic Development, 1972), p. 3.

(16) Ibid., p. 4.

(17) Ibid., pp. 22-23.

(18) Three years ago an UNCTAD consultant studying the fund observed "a relative absence of political discrimination in the choice of recipients." White, Economic Integration, p. 38. The same observation still holds.

(19) Early in 1973 the personal envoy of an Arab president paid a visit to the Gulf states investigating opportunities for financial cooperation. In Kuwait the envoy contacted the fund through the foreign ministry in regard to some projects the fund had rejected. The envoy was told that the fund would not reverse its decision but would look into new opportunities for cooperation.

(20) Stephens, p. 48.

(21) Ibid., p. 55.

(22) Abdlatif Al-Hamad, Bilateral Development Aid: The View from the Kuwait Fund (Kuwait: The Kuwait Fund for Arab Economic Development, 1974), p. 9.

(23) Ibid.

(24) Articles 13 and 14 of the charter of the Kuwait Fund for Arab Economic Development.

(25) Program loans is the term referring to loans "meant to finance import requirements associated with a fairly detailed program of investment that has been reviewed by the lender agency." Raymond F. Mikesell, Public International Lending for Development (New York: Random House, 1966), p. 33.

(26) Raymond F. Mikesell, The Economics of Foreign Aid (Chicago: Aldine, 1968), p. 171.

(27) A recent study on problems of project identification in developing countries could cite only Egypt and Lebanon (among the Arab countries) where some form of project identification units exist on a small scale. See Dennis A. Rondinelli "Project Identification in Economic Development," Journal of World Trade Law 10 (May-June 1976): 233-4.

(28) Al-Hamad, Bilateral Development Aid, p.7.

(29) The Kuwait Fund for Arab Economic Development, Annual Report 1974-1975, p. 39.

(30) Abdlatif Al-Hamad, Towards Closer Economic Cooperation in the Middle East: Financial Aspects (Kuwait: The Kuwait Fund for Arab Economic Development, 1975); The Middle East's Economic Aspirations and the United States (Kuwait: The Kuwait Fund for Arab Economic Development, 1975); Multilateral Investments and Arab Economic Integration (Kuwait: The Kuwait Fund for Arab Economic Development, 1974) (in Arabic).

(31) A possible line of development for the Kuwait Fund is to emphasize its role as a foreign aid agency dispensing economic assistance to the poorer countries of Asia, Africa, and Latin America. This would result in a less active role played by the Fund in Arab regional development and economic integration; see The Washington Post, July 15, 1976, p. A18. However, for reasons mentioned above and elaborated in Chapter 4, we think the fund's regional role would be more rather than less vigorous.

CHAPTER 2

(1) Law No. 3 (1971), Article 3. The successive laws governing the Abu Dhabi Fund are published in a document available from the fund, entitled The Abu Dhabi Fund for Arab Economic Development: Law and Regulations. (See Appendix C)

(2) Ibrahim Shihata, "Arab Development Financing Institutions," International Politics Quarterly 11 (October 1975): 124 (in Arabic).

(3) Law No. 3 (1971), Article 2. As will be shown later, these broad terms of reference for the fund's work were to serve a political function.

(4) White, Economic Integration, p. 44.

(5) Law No. 7 (1974), Article 2.

(6) White, Economic Integration, p. 47.

(7) Ibid.

(8) Ragaei El-Mallakh and Mihssen Kadhim, "Arab Institutionalized Development Aid: An Evaluation," Middle East Journal 30 (Autumn 1976): 477.

(9) Shihata, p. 124.

(10) The grant element is calculated by discounting future repayment of loans using 10% discount rate (including amortization and repayment of interest) and subtracting it from the face value of the loan; see J. White, The Politics of Foreign Aid (New York: St. Martin's Press, 1974), p. 158. The discount rate used should reflect the market interest rate. The 10% discount rate is used in OECD and World Bank calculations of the grant element in loans.

(11) Hassan M. Selim, "Abu Dhabi Fund for Arab Economic Development," mimeographed, p. 2. This mimeograph is extraced from Hassan M. Selim, "Surplus Funds and Regional Development," in Energy and Development, eds. Ragaei El-Mallakh and Carl McGuire (Boulder, Colo.: University of Colorado, International Research Center for Energy and Economic Development, 1974), Chapter 11.

CHAPTER 3

(1) Article 7 of the Agreement Establishing the Arab Fund for Economic and Social Development. The text of the articles of agreement was published in Arabic and English as an Arab Fund document.

(2) Ibid., Article 22.

(3) Ibid., Article 21.

(4) White, Economic Integration, p. 51.

(5) The World Bank experience shows that a president in such an organization has to have considerable power in running the organization in order to achieve any degree of effectiveness in operations; cf. Edward S. Mason and Robert E. Asher, The World Bank Since Bretton Woods (Washington: The Brookings Institution, 1973), pp. 46-52.

(6) Article 21 of the Agreement Establishing the Arab Fund.

(7) Address by His Excellency, Abdul-Rahman Al-Atiqi, chairman of the board of governors, at the second annual meeting of the board of governors of the Arab Fund for Economic and Social Development, April 1973 (Kuwait: The Arab Fund, 1973), pp. 3-5 (in Arabic).

(8) Article 21 of the Agreement Establishing the Arab Fund.

(9) John White, The Politics of Foreign Aid (New York: St. Martin's Press, 1974), p. 54.

(10) The Arab Fund Annual Report 1974, p. 4.

(11) An elaboration of possible regional roles for the Arab Fund is found in Chapter 4.

(12) Joint financing means that the cofinanciers share in financing the same list of imports connected with a specific phase of the project construction; parallel financing means that the cofinanciers finance separate lists of imports, each list relating to a different aspect of the project construction.

(13) The loan of KD 4 million to the Yemen Arab Republic for the electric power generating plant covers 85% of the project's total cost and 100% of its foreign exchange requirements. In this case the fund financing covers some of the local cost of the project.

(14) This point was discussed in detail in Chapter 2.

(15) The Arab Fund Annual Report 1974, p. 5.

(16) Article 2 of the Agreement Establishing the Arab Fund.

(17) The Arab Fund Annual Report 1974, p. 6.

(18) See UNCTAD, Financial Cooperation between OPEC and other Developing Countries (TD/B/AC.19/R.8/Add.1), October 1975, p. 70. A detailed discussion of the program is found in Chapter 4.

(19) Hossein Askari and J. Thomas Cummings, Middle East Economies in the 1970s: A Comparative Approach (New York: Praeger, 1976), p. 100.

(20) For a recent report on AAAID, see Al-Iktisad Al-Arabi, 22 (April 1978): 57 (in Arabic).

CHAPTER 4

(1) Advocates of Arab integration emphasize joint aspirations as the paramount factor behind contemporary efforts to articulate Arab regional identity in economic and political terms.

(2) Ragaei El-Mallakh, "Industrialization in the Arab World: Obstacles and Prospects," in Arab Oil: Impact on the Arab Countries and Global Implications, eds. Naiem A. Sherbini and Mark A. Tessler (New York: Praeger, 1976), p. 71.

(3) Charles Pentland, "The Regionalization of World Politics: Concepts and Evidence," International Journal XXX (Autumn 1975): 602.

(4) Samir Amin, "The Third World and the New Economic Order," Cultures III (No. 4, 1976): 62-3.

(5) Ibid., p. 65.

(6) Report of the Secretary General to the Twenty-Seventh Regular Session of the Council for Arab Economic Unity, Cairo, June 1976, pp. 57-8 (in Arabic).

(7) A recent review of the effects of the Arab Common Market on the promotion of trade among its members and on the dynamics of regional economic changes concluded that ACM did not have any substantial positive effects. See Hossein Askari and J.T. Cummings, Middle East Economics in the 1970s, pp. 409-16.

(8) See the text of the agreement in Alfred G. Musrey, An Arab Common Market: A Study in Inter-Arab Trade Relations, 1920-67 (New York: Praeger, 1969), pp. 178-84.

(9) Ibid., p. 112.

(10) Lynn K. Mytelka, "The Salience of Gains in Third-World Integrative Systems," World Politics 25 (January 1973): 240-45.

(11) Galal A. Amin, The Modernization of Poverty: A Study in the Political Economy of Growth in Nine Arab Countries, 1945-1970, (Leiden: E.J. Brill, 1974), pp. 32-3.

(12) Felipe Pazos, "Regional Integration of Trade Among Less Developed Countries," World Development 1 (July 1973): 9-10.

(13) Alfred Musrey, p. 144.

(14) H. Kitamura, "Economic Theory and the Economic Integration of Underdeveloped Regions," in M.S. Wionczek, ed., Latin American Economic Integration: Experiences and Prospects (New York: Praeger, 1966), p. 44.

(15) Mytelka, p. 246.

(16) Bela Balassa and Andy Stoutjesdijk, "Economic Integration Among Developing Countries," (Washington: World Bank Staff Working Paper No. 186, September 1974, mimeographed). Also, Jan Tinbergen, International Economic Integration (New York: American Elsevier Company, 1965).

(17) G. Amin, p. 33.

(18) L.B.M. Mennes, Planning Economic Integration Among Developing Countries (Rotterdam: University of Rotterdam Press, 1972).

(19) UNCTAD, Current Problems of Economic Integration: The Role of Multilateral Financial Institutions in Promoting Integration Among Developing Countries (TD/B/531), 1975, Sales No. E.75.II.D.5, p. 18.

(20) John White, "International Agencies: The Case for Proliferation," in Gerald H. Helleiner, ed., A World Divided: The Less Developed Countries in the International Economy, (Cambridge: Cambridge University Press, 1976), pp. 285-6.

(21) The theory of regional integration and cooperation among social units stresses the aspect of social learning, or socialization of elites, that occurs in successful examples of cooperation. Such socialization or social learning can be utilized at later stages to enhance the cooperative experience; cf. Ernest Haas, "The Study of Regional Integration," International Organization 24 (Autumn 1970).

(22) George Tomeh, "OAPEC: Its Growing Role in Arab and World Affairs," The Journal of Energy and Development III (Autumn 1977): 33-4.

(23) For a discussion of such procedures, see Dennis A. Rondinelli, "Project Identification in Economic Development," Journal of World Trade Law 10 (May-June 1976).

(24) Mason and Asher, The World Bank Since Bretton Woods, p. 308.

(25) El-Mallakh and Kadhim, Arab Development Aid, pp. 482-3.

(26) Gouda Abdel-Khalek, "Toward One Arab Fund for Economic Development," International Politics 13 (April 1977). (In Arabic).

(27) For a discussion of this point in the context of the Kuwait Fund, see Soliman Demir, The Kuwait Fund, Chapter 2, especially pp. 21-7.

(28) John Percival, Oil Wealth: Middle East Spending and Investment Patterns (New York and London: The Financial Times Limited, May 1975), p. 70.

(29) White, The Case for Proliferation, p. 284.

(30) Gouda Abdel-Khalek, pp. 91-2.

(31) Ibid, p. 93.

(32) El-Mallakh and Kadhim, Arab Development Aid, p. 483.

(33) Soliman Demir, "Arab Regional Integration and Trilateral Cooperation," in Special Approaches to Trilateral Co-operation: Proceedings and Background Papers of the Conference Organised by OECD on 26-27 January, 1977. (Paris: OECD Development Centre, 1978), p. 190.

(34) Hossein Askari and J. Thomas Cummings, Middle East Economies in the 1970s, p. 426.

(35) Robert L. Rothstein, "Politics and Policy-Making in the Third World: Does a Reform Strategy Make Sense?" World Development 4 (August 1976): 695.

(36) Jagdish N. Bhagwati, "Economics and World Order from the 1970s to the

1990s: The Key Issues," in Economics and World Order: From the 1970s to the 1990s, ed., Jagdish N. Bhagwati (New York: Macmillan, 1972), p. 12.

(37) UNCTAD, Economic Cooperation Among Developing Countries: Report by the UNCTAD Secretariat. (TD/192), May 1976, p. 5.

(38) ECOSOC, Highlights of over-all review of growth performance and sectoral trends and development issues in countries of Western Asia. (E/5692), May 1975, p. 14.

(39) The Kuwait Fund Annual Report 1975/1976, p. 74.

(40) ECWA, Follow-up Action on the Resolution Adopted by the Commission at its Third Session in May 1976. (E/ECWA/48), March 1977, p. 9.

(41) United Nations Office of Public Information, Press Release ECWA/34, May 2, 1977.

(42) See UNDP document REM/74/011/A/01/46, concerning Program for the Identification and Preparation of Intercountry Investment Projects and Related Feasibility Studies.

(43) Ibid., p. 12

(44) UNCTAD, "Program for the Identification and Preparation of Inter-country Investment Projects and Related Feasibility Studies: Manual for Multicountry Project Identification, Preparation and Evaluation in the Arab Countries" (mimeographed).

(45) ECWA in cooperation with FAO has sponsored a study for the purpose of devising policies to increase food production in the region; see ECOSOC, Short-Term Possibilities for Increasing Food Production in Selected Countries of the ECWA Region, March 1977.

(46) See Table 2 in Roger A. Hornstein, "Cofinancing of Bank and IDA Projects," Finance and Development 14 (June 1977): 43.

(47) UNDP, Country and Intercountry Programming and Projects: Regional Program for Europe, Mediterranean, and the Middle East, 1977-1981. (DP/218), October 1976, p. 10.

(48) Abdlatif Al-Hamad, Arab Funds and International Economic Cooperation (Kuwait: The Kuwait Fund, November 1973), p. 4.

Selected Bibliography

OFFICIAL DOCUMENTS AND REPORTS

Arab Sources

Abu Dhabi Fund for Arab Economic Development. First Annual Report 1974-1975.

The Arab Fund for Economic and Social Development. Agreement Establishing the Arab Fund for Economic and Social Development, 1968.

The Arab Fund for Economic and Social Development. Annual Reports 1973 and 1974.

Council for Arab Economic Unity. Report of the Secretary-General to the Twenty-Seventh Regular Session of the Council for Arab Economic Unity. Cairo, June 1976 (in Arabic).

The Emirate of Abu Dhabi. Establishment of Abu Dhabi Fund for Arab Economic Development. Law No. (3), 1971.

The Emirate of Abu Dhabi. Amendment of Provisions of Law (3) 1971, Establishing the Abu Dhabi Fund for Arab Economic Development. Law No. (7) 1974.

The State of Kuwait. Law Establishing the Kuwait Fund for Arab Economic Development. Law No. (35) 1961.

The State of Kuwait. The Reorganization of the Kuwait Fund for Arab Economic Development. Law No. (25) 1974.

The Kuwait Fund for Arab Economic Development. Annual Reports 1963/64-1976/77.

Other Sources

Organization for Economic Cooperation and Development. Development Cooperation: 1975 Review. Paris: OECD, November 1976.

United Nations. Economic Commission for Western Asia. Follow-up Action on the Resolutions Adopted by the Commission at its Third Session in May 1976. (E/ECWA/48), March 1977.

United Nations. Economic and Social Council, Highlights of over-all review of growth performance and sectoral trends and development issues in countries of Western Asia. (E/5692), May 1975.

United Nations. Economic and Social Council, Short-term Possibilities for Increasing Food Production in Selected Countries of the ECWA region. March 1977.

United Nations Conference on Trade and Development. Current Problems of Economic Integration: The Role of Multilateral Financial Institutions in Promoting Integration Among Developing Countries. (TD/B/531), 1975. Sales No. E.75.II.D.5.

United Nations Conference on Trade and Development. Financial Cooperation Among Developing Countries: Financial Cooperation Between OPEC and Other Developing Countries. (TD/B/AC.19/R.8/Add. 1), October 1975.

United Nations Conference on Trade and Development. Economic Cooperation Among Developing Countries: Report by the UNCTAD Secretariat. (TD/192), May 1976.

United Nations Conference on Trade and Development. "Program for the Identification and Preparation of Intercountry Investment Projects and Related Feasibility Studies: Manual for Multicountry Project Identification, Preparation, and Evaluation in the Arab Countries" (mimeograhed).

United Nations Development Program. Program for the Identification and Preparation of Intercountry Investment Projects and Related Feasibility Studies. (REM/74/11/011/A/01/46).

United Nations Development Program. Country and Intercountry Programming and Projects: Regional Program for Europe, Mediterranean, and the Middle East, 1977-1981. (DP/218) October 1976.

United Nations Development Program. Report by the Administrator for 1976. (DP/255).

ARTICLES, BOOKS, AND PAPERS

Abdel Khalek, Gouda. "Toward One Arab Fund for Economic Development." International Politics Quarterly 13 (April 1977): 78-94 (in Arabic).

Al-Hamad, Abdlatif. The Kuwait Fund. Kuwait: The Kuwait Fund for Arab Economic Development, February 1971 (in Arabic).

_____. Building Up Development-Oriented Institutions in the Arab Countries. Kuwait: The Kuwait Fund for Arab Economic Development, October 1972.

_____. Arab Funds and International Economic Cooperation. Kuwait: The Kuwait Fund, November 1973.

_____. Bilateral Development Aid: The View from the Kuwait Fund. Kuwait: The Kuwait Fund, January 1974.

_____. Multilateral Investment and Arab Economic Integration. Kuwait: The Kuwait Fund, December 1974 (in Arabic).

_____. The Middle East's Economic Aspirations and the United States. Kuwait: The Kuwait Fund, September 1975.

_____. Towards Closer Economic Cooperation in the Middle East: Financial Aspects. Kuwait: The Kuwait Fund, October 1975.

Amin, Galal A. The Modernization of Poverty: A Study in the Political Economy of Growth in Nine Arab Countries, 1945-1970. Leiden: E.J. Brill, 1974.

Amin, Samir, "The Third World and the New Economic Order." Cultures III (No. 4, 1976): 58-65.

Andic, Fuat; Andic S.; and Dosser, D. A Theory of Economic Integration for Developing Countries. London: George Allen and Unwin, 1971.

Asher, Robert E. "International Agencies and Economic Development: An Overview." International Organization 22 (Winter 1968): 423-58.

Askari, Hossein, and Cummings, J. Thomas. Middle East Economies in the 1970s: A Comparative Approach. New York: Praeger, 1976.

Baer, Werner. "The World Bank Group and the Process of Socio-Economic Development in the Third World." World Development 2 (June 1974); 1-10.

Balassa, Bela. "Toward a Theory of Economic Integration." in Latin American Economic Integration: Experiences and Prospects, pp. 21-31. Ed., Miguel S. Wionczek. New York: Praeger, 1966.

_____, and Stoutjesdijk, Andy. "Economic Integration Among Developing Countries." Washington: World Bank Staff Working Paper No. 186, September 1974 (mimeographed).

Balogh, Thomas. The Economics of Poverty. 2nd Ed. London: Weidenfeld and Nicolson, 1974.

Bhagwati, Jagdish No., ed. Economics and World Order: From the 1970s to the 1990s. New York: Macmillan, 1972.

Colaco, Francis X. Economic and Political Considerations and the Flow of Official Resources to Developing Countries. Paris: OECD Development Centre, 1973.

Cooper, Richard N. "A New International Economic Order for Mutual Gain." Foreign Policy, No. 26 (Spring 1977): 66-120.

Demir, Soliman. The Kuwait Fund and the Political Economy of Arab Regional Development. New York: Praeger, 1976.

_____. "Arab Regional Integration and Trilateral Cooperation." In Special Approaches to Trilateral Cooperation: Proceedings and Background Papers of the Conference Organized by OECD on January 26-27, 1977, pp. 179-192. Paris: OECD Development Center, 1978.

Dexter, L.A. Elite and Specialized Interviewing. Evanston, Ill. Northwestern University Press, 1970.

El-Mallakh, Ragaie. "Industrialization in the Arab World: Obstacles and Prospects." In Arab Oil: Impact on Arab Countries and Global Implications, pp. 58-74. Ed., Naiem A. Sherbini and Mark A. Tessler. New York: Praeger, 1976.

_____, and Kadhim, M. "Arab Institutionalized Development Aid: An Evaluation." Middle East Journal 30 (Autumn 1976): 471-84.

Grunwald, J., et al. Latin American Economic Integration and U.S. Policy. Washington: The Brookings Institution, 1972.

Haas, Ernest B. "The Study of Regional Integration." International Organization 24 (Autumn 1970): 607-46.

_____. The Obsolescence of Regional Integration Theory. Berkeley, California: University of California Institute for International Studies, 1975.

Haq, Mahbub, Ul. The Poverty Curtain: Choices for the Third World. New York: Columbia University Press, 1976.

Hornstein, Roger A. "Cofinancing of Bank and IDA Projects." Finance and Development 14 (June 1977): 40-44.

Kahnert, F., et al. Economic Integration Among Developing Countries. Paris: OECD Development Center, 1969.

Kane, Joseph A. Development Banking. Lexington, Mass.: Heath, 1975.

Kitamura, Hiroshi. "Economic Theory and the Economic Integration of Underdeveloped Regions." In Latin American Economic Integration: Experiences and Prospects, pp. 42-63. Ed., Miguel S. Wionczek. New York: Praeger, 1966.

Lal, Deepak. Appraising Foreign Investment in Developing Countries. London: Hienemann, 1975.

Lipsey, R.G. The Theory of Customs Unions: A General Equilibrium Analysis. London: Wiedenfeld and Nicolson, 1970.

Mason, Edward S., and Asher, R.E. The World Bank Since Bretton Woods. Washington: The Brookings Institution, 1973.

Mennes, L.B.M. Planning Economic Integration Among Developing Countries. Rotterdam: University of Rotterdam Press, 1972.

Mikesell, Raymond. Public International Lending for Development. New York: Random House, 1966.

_____. The Economics of Foreign Aid. Chicago: Aldine, 1968.

Musrey, Alfred G. An Arab Common Market: A Study in Inter-Arab Trade Relations, 1920-67. New York: Praeger, 1969.

Mwine, Frank A. "Co-Financing and Cooperation Between Arab Development Institutions and the World Bank Group." Washington: World Bank, January 1978 (mimeographed).

Mytelka, L.K. "The Salience of Gains in Third World Integration Systems." World Politics 25 (January 1973): 236-50.

Nasr, Z., and El-Khoja, M. Report on Arab Industrial Development Banks. Kuwait: The Kuwait Fund for Arab Economic Development, 1972.

Pazos, Felipe. "Regional Integration of Trade Among Less Developed Countries." World Development 1 (July 1973): 1-12.

Pentland, Charles. "The Regionalization of World Politics: Concepts and Evidence." International Journal XXX (Autumn 1975): 599-630.

Percival, John. Oil Wealth: Middle East Spending and Investment Patterns. New York and London: The Financial Times Limited, May 1975.

Rondinelli, Dennis A. "Project Identification in Economic Development." Journal of World Trade Law 10 (May-June 1976): 215-51.

Rothstein, Robert L. "Politics and Policy-Making in the Third World: Does a Reform Strategy Make Sense?" World Development 4 (August 1976): pp. 695-708.

_____. The Weak in the World of the Strong: The Developing Countries in the International System. New York: Columbia University Press, 1977.

Rustow, Dankwart A., and Mugno, J.F. OPEC: Success and Prospects. New York: New York University Press, 1976.

Scharf, Traute. Arab Development Funds and Banks: Approaches to Trilateral Cooperation. Paris: OECD Development Center, 1978.

Selim, Hassan M. "Abu Dhabi Fund for Arab Economic Development." Extracted from H.M. Selim, "Surplus Funds and Regional Development." In Energy and Development. Eds., Ragaie El-Mallakh and Carl McGuire. Boulder, Colo.: International Research Center for Energy and Economic Development, University of Colorado, 1974.

_____. "Aid Process: The Experience of Abu Dhabi Fund for Arab Economic Development." Paper submitted to UNCTAD meeting on Bilateral and Multilateral Financial and Technical Assistance Institutions. Geneva, March 14-22, 1977.

Shihata, Ibrahim. "Arab Development Financing Institutions." International Politics Quarterly 11 (October 1975): 119-31 (in Arabic).

_____, and Mabro, R. The OPEC Aid Record. Vienna: The OPEC Special Fund, January 1978.

Sideri, Sandro. "Some Notes on UNCTAD IV." Development and Change 7 (October 1976): 485-95.

Stephens, Robert. The Arabs' New Frontier. London: Temple Smith, 1973.

Syz, John. International Development Banks. New York: Oceana, 1974.

Thompson, James D., et al. Comparative Studies in Administration. Pittsburgh: University of Pittsburgh Press, 1959.

Tinbergen, Jan. International Economic Integration. New York: American Elsevier, 1965.

Tomeh, George. "OAPEC: Its Growing Role in Arab and World Affairs." The Journal of Energy and Development III (Autumn 1977): 26-36.

Viner, Jacob. The Customs Union Issue. New York: Carnegie Endowment for International Peace, 1950.

White, John. Promotion of Economic Integration Through Development Finance Institutions: Three Case Studies. UNCTAD Publications, (TAD/EI/MFI/2), February 1974.

_____. The Politics of Foreign Aid. New York: St. Martin's Press, 1974.

_____. "International Agencies: The Case for Proliferation." In A World Divided: The Less Developed Countries in the International Economy, pp. 275-93. Edited by Gerald H. Helleiner. Cambridge: Cambridge University Press, 1976.

Index

129

About the Author

SOLIMAN DEMIR is a Research Associate at the United Nations Institute for Training and Research (UNITAR). He was previously on the staff of the National Bank of Egypt, the National Center for Social Research and the National Institute for Management Development in Cairo.

In addition to publications in English which include The Kuwait Fund and the Political Economy of Arab Regional Development (Praeger, 1976), and "Arab Regional Integration and Trilateral Cooperation" in Special Approaches to Trilateral Cooperation (Paris: OECD, 1978), Dr. Demir has published articles in Arabic in the Egyptian periodicals Management Quarterly, International Politics, and Economist Al-Ahram.

Dr. Demir holds B.A. and M.S. degrees from Cairo University, an M.A. from the American University of Beirut, and a Ph.D. from the University of Pittsburgh.

Pergamon Policy Studies